LITERATURE FROM CRESCENT MOON PUBLISHING

Sexing Hardy: Thomas Hardy and Feminism
by Margaret Elvy

Thomas Hardy's Jude the Obscure: A Critical Study
by Margaret Elvy

Thomas Hardy's Tess of the d'Urbervilles: A Critical Study
by Margaret Elvy

Stepping Forward: Essays, Lectures and Interviews
by Wolfgang Iser

Andrea Dworkin
by Jeremy Robinson

German Romantic Poetry: Goethe, Novalis, Heine, Hölderlin
by Carol Appleby

Rilke: Space, Essence and Angels in the Poetry of Rainer Maria Rilke
by B.D. Barnacle

D.H. Lawrence: Symbolic Landscapes
by Jane Foster

Samuel Beckett Goes Into the Silence
by Jeremy Robinson

In the Dim Void: Samuel Beckett's Late Trilogy: Company, Ill Seen, Ill Said and Worstward Ho
by Gregory Johns

Andre Gide: Fiction and Fervour
by Jeremy Robinson

Amorous Life: John Cowper Powys and the Manifestation of Affectivity
by H.W. Fawkner

Postmodern Powys: New Essays on John Cowper Powys
by Joe Boulter

Rethinking Powys: Critical Essays on John Cowper Powys
edited by Jeremy Robinson

Thomas Hardy and John Cowper Powys: Wessex Revisited
by Jeremy Robinson

Julia Kristeva: Art, Love, Melancholy, Philosophy, Semiotics
by Kelly Ives

Luce Irigaray: Lips, Kissing, and the Politics of Sexual Difference
by Kelly Ives

Helene Cixous I Love You: The Jouissance of Writing
by Kelly Ives

Emily Dickinson: *Selected Poems*
selected and introduced by Miriam Chalk

Petrarch, Dante and the Troubadours: The Religion of Love and Poetry
by Cassidy Hughes

Dante: *Selections From the Vita Nuova*
translated by Thomas Okey

Friedrich Hölderlin: *Selected Poems*
translated by Michael Hamburger

Rainer Maria Rilke: *Selected Poems*
translated by Michael Hamburger

Walking In Cornwall
by Ursula Le Guin

D.H. Lawrence

D.H. Lawrence
Infinite Sensual Violence:
Love, Sex and Relationships

Jane Foster

CRESCENT MOON

CRESCENT MOON PUBLISHING
P.O. Box 1312, Maidstone
Kent, ME14 5XU,
Great Britain
www.crmoon.com

First published 1994. Second edition 2008. Third edition 2012. Fourth edition 2020.
© Jane Foster 1994, 2008, 2012, 2020.

Set in Rotis Serif 9 on 13pt.
Designed by Radiance Graphics.

The right of Jane Foster to be identified as the author of this book has been asserted generally in accordance with sections 77 and 78 of the Copyright, Designs and Patents Act 1988.

All rights reserved. No part of this book may be reprinted or reproduced, stored in a retrieval system, or transmitted, in any form or by any means, electronic, mechanical, photocopying, recording or otherwise, without permission from the publisher.

British Library Cataloguing in Publication data

Foster, Jane
D.H. Lawrence: Infinite Sensual Violence
I. Title
823.912

ISBN-13 9781861717757

Contents

Acknowledgements 9

Introduction: The Myth and Legend of D.H. Lawrence 13
1 Love and Sexuality 28
2 D.H. Lawrence's (Sex) Symbols 40
3 Infinite Sensual Violence: *The Rainbow* 57
4 Being Reborn 100
5 *Lady Chatterley's Lover* 112
6 *The Escaped Cock* 133
7 Sex and Death: *Women in Love* 140
8 Sex in the Fiction 154
9 Conclusion 166

Bibliography 171

ABBREVIATIONS

WP	*The White Peacock*
SL	*Sons and Lovers*
R	*The Rainbow*
WL	*Women in Love*
AR	*Aaron's Rod*
LG	*The Lost Girl*
K	*Kangaroo*
PS	*The Plumed Serpent*
FLC	*The First Lady Chatterley*
JTLJ	*John Thomas and Lady Jane*
LCL	*Lady Chatterley's Lover*
CSS	*Collected Short Stories*
CSN	*The Complete Short Novels*
CP	*The Complete Poems*
P1	*Phoenix*
P2	*Phoenix II*
SP	*A Selection from Phoenix*
TH	*Study of Thomas Hardy and Other Essays*
SE	*Selected Essays*
SLC	*Selected Literary Criticism*
F	*Fantasia of the Unconscious*
A	*Apocalypse*
MM	*Mornings in Mexico and Etruscan Places*
TI	*Twilight in Italy*
Moore	*The Collected Letters of D.H. Lawrence*, ed. H.T. Moore
Hux	*The Letters of D.H. Lawrence*, ed. A. Huxley
Let	*The Letters of D.H. Lawrence*, ed. J.T. Boulton

D.H. Lawrence in 1915

D.H. Lawrence, c. 1920

Introduction:

The Myth and Legend of the Priest of Love

Personality Cult

D.H. Lawrence (September 11, 1885 – March 2, 1930) spawned more versions of himself than many other writers. There are the Lawrences in the works: the poet, playwright, correspondent, novelist, painter, travel writer, historian, critic and psychologist. In his artistic output, and in criticism since, Lawrence plays a number of roles: sociologist, Marxist, traveller, prophet, literary critic, feminist, mystic, martyr, politician, folklorist, theologian, agony aunt, hippy, genius, liar, fascist, Midlander, poet, pantheist and chronicler.

   It's not unusual for a writer to tackle many formats: Lawrence Durrell wrote plays, poems, travel books, novels, letters and also painted (D.H. Lawrence also used those forms, including painting). But Lawrence has received more critical attention than most modern British authors. He is in the William Shakespeare, Thomas Hardy and Charles Dickens league. Aside from Shakespeare and Samuel Beckett, there seem to be more books, articles and conferences on Lawrence than anyone else. Keith Sagar's *A D.H. Lawrence Handbook* lists 500 items in its bibliography, up to 1979. Since then the number has grown even more massively (the 50 and 60 year after-death celebrations of 1980 and 1990, for example). Conferences and festivals of Lawrence continue to thrive; there are Lawrence Societies in Japan, U.S.A., Oz and G.B. (among others); Lawrence journals (*Journal of D.H. Lawrence Studies*); a Research Centre; and a strong presence in Nottinghamshire (at the birthplace and university).

In the arena of film and TV, we've had British Broadcasting Corporation TV versions of *Sons and Lovers* (1981), *Lady Chatterley's Lover* (1993), and *The Rainbow* (1988), a Ken Russell *The Rainbow* (1989), an Australian *Kangaroo* (1986), *The Priest of Love* (1981), about Lawrence's life, the centenary celebrations in 1985, the dreadful Independent Television *Sons and Lovers,* soft porn films of *Lady Chatterley's Lover* (1981) and *The Young Lady Chatterley* (1989, plus a sequel), and *Women In Love* (2011), etc. (D.H. Lawrence's popularity in the cinema was really launched by United Artists' *Women In Love* adaption of 1969; other films of the time included the North American versions of *The Fox* (1968), and *The Virgin and the Gipsy* (1970).)

Like Thomas Hardy and William Shakespeare, D.H. Lawrence is an industry, a cultural icon, the subject of TV, radio, magazines, films, vacations, tours, lectures, courses, festivals, shops, cafés, walks, etc. The tourist industry exalts the rural Lawrence, the homeboy who made good but never forgot his roots (his final novel is set there). The general public exalts the social geographer, politely ignoring his violent rants, his sometimes bizarre philosophies (such as of blood and race), his flirtations with fascist ideology, and his attacks on institutions such as marriage, the Church, religion, education and Britain. Thomas Hardy is much easier to market in some respects: 'Hardy's Wessex' – how lovely and rustic and homely it is, re-affirming bourgeois attitudes. Not so Lawrence, born into the grim and grimy East Midlands. Beauty is harder to find there – or at least the easily packaged, inoffensive, marketable kind of beauty beloved of the media and bourgeosie since Victorian times.

One of the main attractions of D.H. Lawrence Land – it's the same with Thomas Hardy, Jane Austen and Emily Brontë – is love. It's his central subject. When he writes of love he can weave in just about anything he likes. Love – or the better terms 'relationship' or 'romance' – makes Lawrence popular (his stories are romances, or relationship tales).

D.H. Lawrence's fiction stands at the centre of his work, not his travel books, his letters, his plays or poems. It's D.H.L.'s fiction that gets talked about more than anything else (and is adapted more than anything else). Because he tells stories, and people are so hungry for stories (stories continue to dominate global media, secular versions of ancient myths).

D.H. Lawrence is not as simple as this, however. He did not write, as Thomas Hardy did, for a domestic (romantic) fiction magazine market. Lawrence wrote his books in the archetypal modernist fashion: in exile, abroad, uprooted, restlessly travelling. Each book is a stand-alone product, not part of a franchise or series. Each book is meant to be literary (artistic, 'serious') fiction, rather than populist or pulp fiction. Though he constructs most of his art around a story, Lawrence fiction is always psychological, polemical, religious. His target is states of being, primarily, as well as social institutions, religions, materialism, marriage, the Church, education, etc. Reading Lawrence is not to travel neatly from A to Z, in a cause and effect fashion. His stories are in fact very often static, like Samuel Beckett's, or they spiral wildly around the subject, or they attack the same subject from different angles (like the repeated patterns in *Women In Love*). Beckett is the true postmodernist; he does away with story and plot, with just about everything. His characters hobble through dim forests, but the motion is not for story, it parallels the writer at the typewriter. Like Beckett, Lawrence is dynamic, taking ages to explore the ontological states of his characters (he prefers a lot of space, as with James Joyce or John Cowper Powys, in which to spread his wings).

D.H. Lawrence: Infinite Sensual Violence

Reading Lawrence can be difficult. With his simple, rhythmic language he takes you deeper and deeper into the modern soul. You don't know where you are, it's a big space full of conflicts, feelings, ideas, views of all kinds, and always an emphasis on the body and its pulsations, its feelings, its reactions. You have to be in the mood for Lawrence, you might say, as with James Joyce, Virginia Woolf and Samuel Beckett. It's not 'light reading': like the movies of Ingmar Bergman or Jean-Luc Godard, it demands quite a lot more from the consumer than many novels. You have to give a lot to some works of art: but Lawrence's works pay you back. 'Stream of consciousness' is the usual term, but in Lawrence's work streams of being, of feelings, of presences, or of the unconscious, is more accurate.

So why is it he fascinates so many people still, in a way that Italo Svevo, Alain Robbe-Grillet, E.M. Forster and Günter Grass do not, and on such a huge critical scale?

Firstly, there is love and sexuality – you can see D.H. Lawrence developing the tradition of Jane Austen, Thomas Hardy and George Eliot, or you can break him apart as a misogynist, as second wave feminists such as Kate Millett and Andrea Dworkin have done. Or as a wife-beater, as Mary Daly and Katherine Mansfield have done. Or you can write about his positive images of women, or his homosexuality. Then there is sodomy, a favourite subject of modern, European writers. There is the political Lawrence, the utopian visionary, the socialist, and the neo-fascist. The religious Lawrence – endless scope for discussions of Lawrence's beliefs, his paganism, his new Christianity, his Apocalyptical thinking. Lawrence the philosopher, the intuitive explorer of a heap of issues. Lawrence the prolific letter-writer – all those letters to wade through, from the trivial to the profound, all meticulously collected in the Cambridge University Press editions. The traveller: visit the places – how much did he get 'wrong'? The post-Walt Whitman poet. The culture merchant, trading in Friedrich Nietzsche, Fyodor Dostoievsky, Sigmund Freud, the *Bible*. The anti-hero of counter-culture. The socialite (he knew a lot of people). The friend of Bertrand Russell,

D.H. Lawrence: Infinite Sensual Violence

Aldous Huxley, John Middleton Murry, Frieda Lawrence, John Mansfield, Richard Aldington, Lady Ottoline Morrell, etc.

❈

Just about everyone, it seems, has had a go at 'writing' D.H. Lawrence. There are still many D.H. Lawrences to be written. There are many studies of Lawrence, as there are many Lawrences (but there are more Lawrences than studies of Lawrence, and each study creates a new Lawrence). There is no 'definitive' study of Lawrence (though there are core critics, whose tomes form the standard approach to Lawrence's art). This study is only one among many. My own views on Lawrence change, so there is nothing 'final' about this book. Lawrence is one of those writers, like William Shakespeare, who won't remain fixed in any particular interpretation, one of those authors who, as soon as you fix them in one reading, leap out and become something else.

D.H. Lawrence polarizes readers and writers as few other writers do. People either love or hate him. Few are indifferent. In the opinion of many he is the key writer in English of the 20th century. Many writers have been influenced by Lawrence: Anaïs Nin, Henry Miller, Lawrence Durrell, Norman Mailer, Margaret Drabble, Raymond Carver, Richard Aldington, George Orwell, Ted Hughes, W.H. Auden, Charles Bukowski, Anthony Burgess, Robert Creeley, William Carlos Williams, etc. Many people championed Lawrence: F.R. Leavis, Keith Sagar, Aldington, Nin, Miller, Harry Moore. Henry Miller typifies those who love Lawrence: he is a Christ, a hero, a passionate soul, a heroic genius, a visionary, etc. This view – of Lawrence as a heroic genius of love and life – is still held by many today.

For Anaïs Nin, D.H. Lawrence was a brilliant poet of sensuality. She loves him because he wrote about the experience of being a woman; and because he reclaimed women's sexual experiences from obscurity (*Journal* 3, 210-1). For Nin, Lawrence was the re-inventor of poetic realism, and his subject matter was also Nin's – emotional transformation. Of *Lady Chatterley's Lover,* Nin writes in *D.H. Lawrence,* in her usual intuitive way:

A vigorous and impetuous style carries the weight of intense physical and imaginative emotions and in the end unites them in a brilliant fusion of physical-mysticism. (108)

For Richard Aldington, 'both in living and in writing D.H. Lawrence was a genius, but...' (*Portrait*, vi). All the criticism of Lawrence discusses his life as well as his art. His life is fused with his art. Critics have found it impossible to untie the art from the life (even though Lawrence states, 'Trust the tale'). The main critics have all found it necessary to talk about the man as well as the artist: Colin Clarke, F.R. Leavis, Harry T. Moore, Mark Kinkead-Weekes, Mark Spilka, Graham Hough, R.D. Draper, H.M. Daleski, Frank Kermode, Keith Sagar, David Holbrook, Julian Moynahan, F.B. Pinion, Gamini Salgado, John Worthen, etc. (For what it's worth the critics I've found useful are: Sagar, Millett, Salgado, Miller, Nin, Holbrook, Pinion, Gabriel Ben-Ephraim, Peter Balbert, Janice Hubbard, and Sheila Macleod). Lawrence the man has fascinated critics and readers as few other artists have (one thinks of J.M.W. Turner, Vincent van Gogh, Arthur Rimbaud, Lord Byron and Emily Brontë).

Most criticism of D.H. Lawrence does not fail to mention some event or characteristic of his life. Feminists will point out that he was a wife-beater, to support their argument that he was a chauvinist and misogynist. Other critics will point to his relationship with John Middelton Murray as the basis of his homosexual discourses. Even more tiresomely, some critics will note that this or that real-life person was the basis of this or that character (Frieda and Louie Burrows for Ursula, Bertrand Russell for Sir Joshua Matteson, etc). (Kingsley Widmer noted in "The Dialectics of Passion in Lawrence" 'how righteously quaint of the late F.R. Leavis in his three books on Lawrence to turn such erratic writing into perfected art and such passional extremity into normative moralisms' [G. Salgado, 1988, 142]). Leavis normalized Lawrence, dragging him into the mainstream of the 'British tradition' of literature. For David Holbrook (in *A Quest for Love*), Lawrence gets it wrong and *Lady Chatterley's Lover*, exalted by Anaïs Nin as Lawrence's best book, is 'cranky and false' (322). For Norman Mailer in *The Prisoner of Sex,* Lawrence was 'a man more beautiful than we can guess' (110).

Each generation invents D.H. Lawrence anew. In the 1960s Lawrence became a hippy, a beatnik, a liberated Bohemian who advocated 'free love' and back-to-nature eco-friendly politics. In the Seventies, second wave feminists attacked Lawrence and explored his ideological ambiguities. In the 1980s, Lawrence proved to be as popular as ever – there was a flurry of critical activity during the 1985 centenary celebrations. Lawrence's politics and polemics continue to antagonize people, but his fiction remains at the core of his achievement and critical status.

Certainly D.H. Lawrence spent a good deal of time being engaged in reading other writers and in literary debate. He has written much literary criticism, which includes pieces on Thomas Hardy, Herman Melville, Edgar Allan Poe, Walt Whitman, Thomas Mann, V.V. Rozanov and Giovanni Verga. Lawrence has many piquant things to say about criticism and art. One of his most famous sayings was: 'Never trust the artist. Trust the tale.' (SLC, 297) But in many of his essays Lawrence is not describing another artist, but himself (the more he writes about, say, Whitman or Melville, the more he reveals of himself). As books such as *Lady Chatterley's Lover* and *Women In Love* show, Lawrence is a very narcissistic writer. Not for him a detached, cool, objective viewpoint. Despite having such wide-ranging influences, Lawrence is very distinctive. His style is his own. He stands out from other writers. If Lawrence was among ten unseen texts, in some English examination, you'd know which was his straight away. His personality is stamped onto all he writes.

D.H. Lawrence: Infinite Sensual Violence

Is D.H. Lawrence (a) Feminist?

> *We should look as skeptically at feminist descriptions of Lawrence that reduce him to a symbolic Other as we do at patriarchal reductions of women writers... his philosophy breaks away from humanism at precisely the same point that feminism does. He treats the problems that arise from gender identity as the ones most deserving of serious attention. Moreover, he takes as his first priority the articulation of female experience. No wonder Lawrence's work continues to fascinate women.*
>
> Carol Siegel, *Lawrence Among the Women* (6, 18)

The man-woman relationship is D.H. Lawrence's main province, his main obsession, in his fiction, and in much of his philosophical writing. But he is very ambiguous about it, and the role of men and women within it. In this discussion, I am approaching Lawrence's fiction and philosophy, his characters and the views in his stories, but *not* the man himself (besides, is anyone now alive who knew Lawrence personally? He died in 1930).

Some feminists believe it is not for D.H. Lawrence to talk about women's experience (Simone de Beauvoir, 245f). Some feminists see Lawrence as a woman-hater, someone who did not, finally, understand women, who belittled them, who feared them, who misrepresented them, even though he used the material of his women friends in his fiction (H. Simpson, 160; C. Siegel, 9).

I don't think that at all, and who does, now that the heyday of second wave feminism is over? Kate Millett led the way in this sort of attack on D.H. Lawrence, in her 1970 book *Sexual Politics,* although later writers (including me) have questioned Millett's analysis: for Nigel Kelsey, Millett's critical analysis is too simplistic; she relies on the humanist connection between text and author; she makes epistemological errors; her psychology is over-simple. Millett's interpretation of Lawrence had a strong influence, however, although it was far too limited in its approach, making all sorts naïve and unsubstantiated assumptions about what a writer is, what they do, how they work, how they think, what writing is, how writing relates to authors, how readers consume fiction, and how criticism relates to literature. There's no need to go further with demolishing Millett's analysis, because all of the holes in it should be obvious to anyone by now.

Other writers see D.H. Lawrence as an important writer, for, despite the apparent chauvinism, he is sympathetic to feminist causes (of course he wasn't misogynist – and his books, non-fiction as well as fiction, are just as critical of men as of women). Sandra M. Gilbert writes (in "Potent Griselda: "The Ladybird" and the Great Mother"):

> Famously misogynistic and, in rhetoric, fiercely, almost fascistically patri-archal, he is nevertheless the author of books whose very titles – *Sons and Lovers, Women In Love, Lady Chatterley's Lover* – are haunted by female primacy, by the autonomous sexual energy of the goddess. (141)

Much of D.H. Lawrence's ambiguous attitude to women stems from his attitude to his mother, critics claim. He loved her, but also resented her and feared her. In this second wave feminist view, women are often put down in his books – especially in the 'leadership' novels, such as 1922's *Aaron's Rod* (284-9) and *The Plumed Serpent*. Lawrence disliked wilful women (or *said* he did – it's not the same thing), women who think they know what they want. His dramas of love pivot around a battle of wills (as between *The Rainbow*'s Anna and Will, for example). Though he yearned for a union in love, for him, it was dualistic, there was a melting into one but also a separateness (SE, 27). Sometimes, it's true, Lawrence does come out with ridiculous and stupidly sexist remarks (he certainly had a big mouth):

> Of all things, the most fatal to a woman is to have an aim, and be cocksure about it. (SP, 392)

Although he loves women, and wants them to become 'self-responsible', like Ursula Brangwen in *The Rainbow*, D.H.L.'s characters also want to dominate them, to subsume their power, to move in to take over their territory. Lawrence was afraid of women – he said so himself (SP, 422). What does that even mean, though? How can anybody, least of all a super-intelligent author, be 'afraid of women'? That's half the population of Earth!

This fear, in the second wave feminist view, is the root of D.H. Lawrence's resentment of women, which sometimes manifests itself in his work as hate, other times as over-compensation and the urge to control. Thus Birkin always tries to outdo Ursula in their conversations in *Women In Love*. The men who want to become 'Masters' are most obnoxious of all – Mellors, Cipriano, Kangaroo, Aaron. They reject women and are consequently laughable.

'Woman is in flood', wrote D.H. Lawrence (SP, 423), but he hated it really, because he couldn't stop the flood. In his fiction, his narrators disliked the will in women – especially in sex, when the woman asserts her will over the man by using her clitoris to achieve the 'seething, frictional electric' orgasm, as he put it in *The Plumed Serpent* (PS, 459). Lawrence's views on the clitoral orgasm, like his views on masturbation, are junk. They are the product of fear, misunderstanding, and the urge to control every aspect of creative activity.

True, D.H. Lawrence created some powerful female characters – Lou, Mrs Witt, Gudrun, Ursula, Mrs Morel, Kate. But sometimes they reflect the glory of the male in the texts. Women are all too often mirrors, as Virginia Woolf said. Lawrence's female characters can only ever be a man's view of women, never more (in the modernist, humanist view which links authorship and texts, where the gender of the author has an impact on the fiction). Lawrence hated 'universal truths' anyway, and never created a 'universal woman'. He misrepresented women's sexuality in the fiction, as well as their needs, desires and personalities, in the view of second wave feminism. His male characters struggle to realize the feminine in themselves, but they remain, from Paul Morel to Oliver Mellors and the Man Who Died, too domineering. The male charas project their fears, nerves and ideas onto the women. It is the typical *anima* problem of Jungian psychology. There are many times when Lawrence and his narrators cannot hide behind the male characters and steps out and speak for their own selves (this happens with Paul, Aaron, Birkin, Lilly, Cipriano, Mellors and Dionys).

D.H. Lawrence's views on women and feminism were ambiguous and inconsistent; the relation of the author's voice and the 'woman's voice' he tried to create within his fictions is problematic; his notions of gender, essentialism, biology, subjectivity and identity shift uncomfortably about. He was never fully certain of what 'the feminine' was, and how masculinist culture should relate to 'feminine' culture. As Andrea Dworkin wrote in *Right-Wing Women*: 'One simply cannot be both for and against the exploitation of women' (197). Lawrence appears to be both for and against feminism, women's power, and women's spirituality. (Of course, because Lawrence never sits still, and his views are not consistent, but intuitive, imaginative, emotional).

Most problematic for feminism in D.H. Lawrence's *œuvre* is 1928's *Lady Chatterley's Lover*. It seems as if D.H.L. is trying to redress the balance, to exalt women again (after veering too far the other way in the 'leadership' novels). But he ends up exalting their sexuality (Mellors effuses over Connie's body, and emphasizing her breasts, hips and buttocks). Mellors is still a man trying to dominate a woman, seen in the anti-Lawrence, feminist view. The exchange is primarily sexual. This is the really sad thing about the book for feminists. It is a big plea for tenderness, but the means to this tenderness is sex. The first time they make love they have hardly spoken. Mellors put his hand on Connie's flank (120), and makes love to her rapidly. The second time they make love it is similar – a few words then quick tupping on a blanket. Hardly any contact, or tenderness, or sympathy for the other person. Thus, in this way and others, *Lady C* offers plenty of fuel for the anti-Lawrence feminists of the Kate Millett ilk, who can cite such scenes as evidence for the denigration of women in Lawrence's work.

It's such a pity that D.H. Lawrence couldn't show more than just sex at times in *Lady C*. Sex is part of love but not the whole of it. Lawrence's mistake is to place all the emphasis on sex and Connie's reawakening through sex. Thus the 1928 novel is depressing (for anti-Lawrence feminists) as well as exhilarating (for those who love what he was saying about tenderness and love). For the feminists who are critical of Lawrence's fiction, women are degraded, and in unambiguous ways:

> "Cunt! Eh, that's the beauty o' thee, lass!... A woman's a lovely thing, when 'er's deep ter fuck, and cunt's good... Tha's got the nicest arse of anybody... a bit o' cunt an' tenderness... it's cunt-awareness" (LCL, 185, 221, 232, 256, 290)

The problem is Oliver Mellors reduces Connie Chatterley to mere 'cunt'. She is reduced to just a body part that he enjoys occasionally. Mellors (and Lawrence's narrator) exalts sex and forgets the rest of it. In pornography, the words 'fuck' and 'love' are interchangeable. To be 'loved' by a man is to be 'fucked'. This is what happened in the censored version of *Lady Chatterley's Lover*: instead of finding the famous line '[w]e fucked a flame into being', we get '[w]e loved a flame into being' (even though the meaning may be ultimately similar). Despite the amount of sex in *Lady C*, some critics have found the sex scenes mediocre:

> for a novel associated in the public mind almost exclusively with sexuality, *Lady Chatterley's Lover* has also seemed, for many of its critics, curiously unsatisfactory on the subject of sex

complained Lydia Blanchard in "Lawrence, Foucault, and the Language of Sexuality (*Lady Chatterley's Lover*)" (121).

The 1928 novel is in some ways a hymn to Oliver Mellors' penis, as Kate Millett noted in *Sexual Politics* (239). Mellors praises Connie's vagina in order to exalt his penis, in the second wave feminist view. The highpoint of the book, the 'night of sensual passion', and the burning out of the deepest shames, is only made possible by the phallus. This is simply rubbish for anti-Lawrenceans.

> D.H. Lawrence writes vile and stupid essays in which he says the same thing [that women must exist for their husbands, do sex and be sex for their husbands] basically with many references to the divine phallus.

D.H. Lawrence: Infinite Sensual Violence

asserted Andrea Dworkin in *Right-Wing Women* (40). The more D.H. Lawrence insists on the primacy of the phallus, for many feminists, the more ridiculous he becomes. "'I *know* it is the penis which connects us with the stars and the sea and everything'", says Connie (JTLJ, 312). The dialogues between Connie and Hilda about the penis are some of the silliest in Lawrence's output. It's a ludicrous notion. No, it's not the phallus that is primary, if you insist on a biological/ essentialist interpretation, but the womb. Womb if you're a poet, brain if you're a scientist, thumb if you're an anthropologist. Lawrence knew the true primacy of the womb, but he kept denying it.

One of the finest feminist writers of the second wave, Mary Daly, pinpointed the true nature of phallicism (in *Pure Lust*):

> Phallic lust is seen as a fiction of obsession and aggression... As aggression it rapes, dismembers and kills women and all living things within its reach. Phallic lust begets phallocratic society, that is sadosociety, which is in fact, pseudosociety. (1)

D.H. Lawrence is one of the most vociferous advocates of the phallocentric society. Connie must bow down low before the altar of Mellors' penis. No writer could make that scene of phallus-worship in *Lady Chatterley's Lover* work (and no filmmaker has attempted it):

> The sun through the low window sent in a beam, that lit up his thighs and slim belly and the erect phallos, rising darkish and hot-looking from the little cloud of vivid gold-red hair. She was startled and afraid.
> "How strange!" she said slowly. "How strange he stands there! So big! and so dark and so cock-sure! Is he like that?" (218)

D.H. Lawrence has tried to get at the source of life here. He has wrongly targeted the essence as the phallus. Mellors and his ever-ready penis is one of the 'cocks, danglers, pricks, and flashers who keep girls and women intimidated', according to Mary Daly (23).

The best thing Connie can do is take her baby and run. The man already has: that would be a typical anti-Lawrence feminist view. In

Women In Love, Gudrun debunks the phallus – one of the few moments in D.H. Lawrence's fiction where the phallus is denigrated:

> His maleness bores me. Nothing is so boring as the phallus, so inherently stupid and stupidly conceited. Really, the fathomless conceit of these men, it is ridiculous – the little strutters. (563)

I

Love and Sexuality

> *It is the sex warmth alone that makes men and women possible to one another.*
>
> D.H. Lawrence, *The First Lady Chatterley* (217)

> *Of all love poets, we are the love poets. For our religion is loving. To love passionately, but completely, is our one desire.*
>
> D.H. Lawrence, "Georgian Poetry: 1911-1912" (SLC, 75)

The Physiology of Sex

D.H. Lawrence's chief concern in his work is life – more and more of life. But the struggle for a vital, vivid kind of living occurs in love, in relationships, and in particular in romantic/ erotic relationships. Love is one of Lawrence's characters' main means of transcendence. His characters struggle to come into being, as he said of Thomas Hardy's protagonists (a rather generalized notion, but it does describe Lawrence's characters, more than Hardy's). From Cyril in the early novel *The White Peacock* (1911) to Connie in his last novel, *Lady Chatterley's Lover* (1928), all Lawrence's characters grapple with love and lovers. As Eugene Goodheart writes of 1915's *The Rainbow* in

Desire and Its Discontents:

> each successive generation, Tom and Lydia, Will and Anna Brangwen, Ursula and Anton Skrebensky shows the self-destructive course of passion, the only alternative to which is self-responsibility, autonomous being, a kind of paradise regained. (64)

D.H. Lawrence's ideas of love were not new – they are traditional Western, Judæo-Christian notions. He turned love, as Westerners have done since Plato, into a religion, a cult, a dogma, a mysticism. Like (Christian) mystics such as John of the Cross or Jan Ruysbroeck or Dionysius the Areopagite, Lawrence speaks of love as a becoming, a travelling, a means to transcendence and being. Love for him is relative, joyous, difficult, multiplitic, two-in-one (SE, 24-28). His real theme is the drawing-together of men and women. It is one of the obsessions of the West since earliest times.

Where D.H. Lawrence differs from many modern authors is in his exaltation of the body. One must love 'in entire nakedness of body and spirit', he asserts (Hux, 203). Lawrence hated sex in the head (557), promiscuity (773), sentimental love (SP, 335), and masturbation (SP, 316f). One must have 'a proper reverence for sex', he claimed (331). Sex is holy for Lawrence. Sex begins with the real hungers and needs and joys of the body (334); it is the 'supreme desire' (TH, 56); it flows to 'the very furtherest edge of known feeling' (ib., 52). In the sex act the rivers of blood of the man and woman merge (SP, 350; F, 104). Some of Lawrence's writings on sex sound like a cross between a stern sermon and a wildly inaccurate mediæval book of alchemy:

> In the act of coition, the two seas of blood in the two individuals, rocking and surging towards contact, as near as possible, clash into a oneness. (*Fantasia of the Unconscious*, 104)

Who is D.H. Lawrence addressing here? A class of trainee gynæcologists? A clutch of three-year-olds? A cluster of Biblical patriarchs? Is he lecturing at a Women's Institute, complete with colour photographic slides, each showing blown-up details of these 'rivers of blood'?

The Lawrencean lecture on "The Birth of Sex" (in *Fantasia of the Unconscious*) continues (come on now, you at the back, pay attention!): he says that fullness comes 'when the sex passion submits to the great purposive passion' (F, 108). Love and sex are not everything for Lawrence. There is a beyond-love state. Sometimes it is solitude, sometimes it is a blood-oath sworn with one's brother, as in *Women In Love*. Lawrence wanted to go beyond ordinary love, beyond the passion-and-death scenario (F, 191). But he is very ambivalent about love and sexuality. Sometimes he believes wholly in the mystical union of two people, that two people can become one (TH, 75). This is the Lawrence of *The Rainbow* days (the mid-1910s). He modified his position on this Neoplatonic two-in-oneness later, saying the two rivers still commingle, but retain their separateness (SP, 349). In the late Lawrence (1920s), sex is a vulnerable, delicate, tender thing that is so easily smashed, it must be cultivated. This is Lawrence's view in *Lady Chatterley's Lover*. But he is a Puritan. Too much sex is bad, he says (yet Connie and Mellors are obsessed with sex). Like André Gide and Rainer Maria Rilke (writers of the same era), Lawrence is not an advocate of promiscuous sex. His concept of sex is highly ascetic, despising people who have been 'crucified into sex' (CP, 361). In the 'Tortoise' poems, he wrote of sex as a crucifixion, a primal scream torn from pained reptiles (365-6). In 'He-Goat', Lawrence writes of orgasm-addicts that might be out of William Burroughs' fiction who stink from 'orgasm after orgasm after orgasm' (382).

In D.H. Lawrence's works, sex is sometimes painful, as in the Marquis de Sade and Georges Bataille, *avant garde*, French tradition. In the "Excurse" chapter in *Women In Love*, Ursula and Birkin make love in that highly emotional manner, familiar now because of Lawrence's way of describing it. Unable or unwilling to be specific, to write about what's happening, or about genitals, Lawrence paints bodies clothed in darkness and mystery. It is a form of writing about sex that has been parodied endlessly since *Women and Love* and *Lady Chatterley's Lover* (such as by the brilliant Spike Milligan). Here, Lawrence gives sex a religious treatment:

> They threw off their clothes, and he gathered, lambent reality of her forever invisible flesh. Quenched, inhuman, his fingers upon her unrevealed nudity were the fingers of silence upon silence, the body of mysterious night upon the body of mysterious night, the night masculine and feminine, never to be seen with the eye, or known with the mind, only known as a palpable revelation of mystic otherness.
>
> She had her desire of him, she touched, she received the maximum of unspeakable communication in touch, dark, subtle, positively silent, a magnificent gift and give again, a perfect acceptance and yielding, a mystery, the reality of that which can never be known, mystic, sensual reality that can never be transmuted into mind content, but remains outside, living body of darkness and silence and subtlety, the mystic body of reality. (WL, 403)

Too much sex and too much dwelling on sex is destructive, D.H. Lawrence claims. Yet he fills most of his novels with sex: *Sons and Lovers, The Rainbow, Women In Love, Aaron's Rod, Lady Chatterley's Lover* – these are all books which examine sexual relations in detail. In his essays, too, Lawrence discusses sexuality at great length: the psychology of it, how it works in nature, in symbolism, in emotion.

Many of D.H. Lawrence's notions of sexuality are rubbish. He is wrong about masturbation, homosexuality, abstinence, and promiscuity. His idea that clitoral orgasm (such as Kate's in *The Plumed Serpent*) is harmful and that vaginal orgasm is good (or better) is also junk. He projects his fears idiosyncratically onto the world (as only he could). He makes generalizations out of individual cases. He can be puritanical, old-fashioned, chauvinist, and often hysterical (but he can also be tremendously insightful, perceptive and illuminating).

Sex in Sons and Lovers

D.H. Lawrence's notions of sex are full of ambiguities. He exalts heterosexuality yet pines for a homosexual companion. The homoeroticism in Lawrence's art is very strong in *Aaron's Rod* and *Women In Love*. Lawrence mouths Biblical platitudes, revealing his ignorance of physiology. His narrators and characters can be often severely sexist or even misogynist. Despite exalting women and the Goddess in the *Foreword* to *Sons and Lovers* (Hux, 100f), much of Lawrence's fiction reveals his narrators' distrust and even hatred of women.

Disgust and hate feature highly because, for anti-Lawrencean feminists, D.H. Lawrence fears women. Paul Morel in *Sons and Lovers* is one of the worst offenders. He treats the women in his life abominably. He is patronizing, selfish, spiteful and mistaken. He is very sarcastic with his mother and Miriam (masking his hostility). They have to act as mirrors to reflect his greatness. Part of this Lawrence (and his narrator) is aware of, part of it is (or seems to be) unconscious. At one point he threads together the trinity of women in Paul's psychosexual melodrama: mother, sister and lover: the three women are sitting around him, listening to him read poetry. So great is Paul's arrogance that he thinks they are there for him alone:

> He had got now all the audience he cared for. And Mrs Morel and Annie almost contested with Miriam who should listen and win his favour. (SL, 226)

They'd do better if they told the conceited doofus to go to hell. He doesn't see them or recognize them. They're there, he thinks, to reflect his self-manufactured glory.

The whole of *Sons and Lovers* tends to be like this. At times Paul Morel calls his mother 'blind eye' or 'little woman'. The affectionate terms are really more like the attempts of Paul to get control over his mother. Paul is sly in his passive-aggressive manipulations, his impotence manifesting as frustration and sarcasm. The mother, meanwhile, is far too indulgent with him.

✵

There are moments of bliss in D.H. Lawrence's characters' love-relations, but they are rare. Fighting seems to be more common (or if there is a bliss, it is freighted with ambiguities). The relationship battles, from *The Rainbow* to *The Plumed Serpent*, are intense. In *Women In Love* the Lawrencean male starts to want something more than love.

There is a beyond, argues R. Birkin in *Women In Love*, a separateness (WL, 208-9). Birkin yearns for something beyond marriage and the 'horrible privacy of domestic and connubial satisfaction', which he finds repulsive (269). Ursula throws herself in fully, while Birkin always keeps something back (343). The struggle is not resolved – it continues right up until the very last words of the 1920 book.

Aaron's Rod continues the dialogues about love and relationships of *Women In Love*, though without the artistic fire. The 1922 book is full of desperation and horror and poison (AR, 194). Aaron runs away from his family and former life. A philosophy of solitude is encouraged by Lilly (a Lawrencean mouthpiece) – he harps on about it endlessly (128, 155, 197, 290, 343, etc. Once a Lawrence-preacher gets stuck into a subject that obsesses them, they stubbornly hang on to it for years, and let everybody else know about it, too). So Aaron thanks the universe 'for the blessedness of being alone' (155).

D.H. Lawrence enunciated this love of solitude in his poems and essays. In the poem 'Deeper Than Love', he wrote:

Love is a thing of twoness.
But underneath any twoness, man is alone. (CP, 844)

In *Fantasia of the Unconscious*, he wrote: 'But to be alone with one's own soul! This, and the joy of it, is the real goal of love' (F, 134). This is the modern male talking, who doesn't have children, who has few responsibilities, or old or ill people to look after (i.e., the typical white, European, bourgeois, male hero of Existential fiction, *à la* Jean-Paul

Sartre, André Gide, Knut Hamsun, Albert Camus and Aldous Huxley). Many of D.H. Lawrence's philosophies do not take children into consideration. Like Thomas Hardy, he was childless, and this probably affected his outlook. He could write of the pregnant Anna dancing naked before the fire in one of *The Rainbow*'s stand-out scenes, but he couldn't explore the deeper feelings of pregnancy, childbirth, and rearing children to the same deep degree (if, that is, one wants to pursue a quasi-biographical approach). As Nigel Kelsey comments in *D.H. Lawrence: Sexual Crisis*:

> if we are tempted to lament the absence of a 'real' history it surely has no stronger basis than in the relatively absent signs of childrearing which mark some of the more major silences of the text. (131-2)

There are many children in *The Rainbow*, but the real, authentic experiences of motherhood and child rearing are absent. (Even so, everyone agrees that Bertie Lawrence could write of women, mothers and female characters with more sympathy, insight and perception than most writers, male *or* female). (However, critics talking about 'absences' or 'silences' is curious – it's another instance where a critic is speaking about what they *expect* to find – they imagine that certain ingredients *ought* to be part of the mix. But where in *The Rainbow* is it explicitly stated that child-rearing or domestic responsibilities will be part of the novel? This is, like all of Lawrence's novels, a *relationship* story. If critics complain about things that are 'absent' from a novel, they could have a go at adding those elements themselves. But they never do! They could rewrite *The Rainbow* and put in all of the things they reckon it lacks).

So the Lawrencean male can slink off and be alone, ignoring completely societal, familial, financial and political obligations (like Paul Morel in *Sons and Lovers*, or Oliver Mellors in *Lady C*). Notice, for instance, that few Lawrencean men have to work hard for a living (but that is also a convention of the literary novel genre, just like children in children's stories have to be separated from their parents in order to have adventures). It is a fantasy long harboured by men in literature.

John Cowper Powys is the great exponent of the soul-alone in modern English literature. He surpasses even D.H. Lawrence in this exaltation of Male Escape (in his 1930s novels *Wolf Solent* or *Maiden Castle*, for instance). In *Lady Chatterley*, Lawrence moves back towards the centre of the circle cast by love (although love has also been central to every novel, including the 'wilderness' or 'leadership' novels of the previous years). But the balance in *Lady C*, despite having a female protagonist, is still weighted towards the male. Women have to bow down to phallic religion (symbolized by the erect phallus), as espoused in *Lady Chatterley's Lover*. Women are still subordinate to men in Lawrence's fictional world. The orgasms are extraordinary, and the tenderness is touching, but the biggest transformation comes from anal sex, introducing an ambiguous element to the literary relationship novel.

Anal sex features in much of modern, Western art (outside of pornography): in the Marquis de Sade, Georges Bataille (*The Story of the Eye*), Salvador Dali (his painting *A Young Virgin Sodomized By Her Own Chastity*, for instance), Hans Bellmer (his Surreal drawings of anal penetration), Paul Verlaine and Arthur Rimbaud (in their poem 'Sonnet to the Asshole', for instance), Pauline Reage (*The Story of O*), James Joyce (in *Ulysses*), John Cowper Powys and William Burroughs (Burroughs is probably the King of Anal Sex in modern literature!). Sodomy is an obsession with some writers (French literature and cinema, for instance, is particularly fond of it). It is central to movies such as *Last Tango in Paris, Weekend* and *Salò*. And in contemporary British writers such as Jenny Diski and Martin Amis. Diski's novel *Nothing Natural* directly develops Lawrence's anal metaphysics:

> She felt everything: violated, released, hugely and darkly excited... It went beyond vaginal sex... It was the dark, secret route that took him truly inside her... (30-32)

During the infamous 'night of sensual passion' in *Lady Chatterley's Lover,* anal sex is described in similar terms. It is terrible, thrilling, reckless, shameless. It burns out the 'deepest, oldest shames' (LCL, 258). It is the same with Anna and Will's 'sodomitical activities', as Nigel Kelsey oddly calls them in 1916's *The Rainbow* in his study of Lawrence (134). D.H. Lawrence's sexual ethics focus on the body, as we have said, and for him the bowels and anus, not the phallus nor the womb, are the base of the body, the core of the physical jungle, the last and deepest recess of organic shame (*Lady C,* 259). Much of the 1928 book tackles the politics and materialism of love, and here Lawrence makes the connections, once made by Sigmund Freud, between sex and excrement and gold and bliss in love. Faust in the famous myth was enticed to go down to the foundations of nature, and here Lawrence does the same. (However, Lawrence changes his mind pretty often – this week it's the bowels, but next week it might be the body itself, or the phallus, or the womb as the Fundament of All Life).

The ritual buggery in *Lady Chatterley's Lover* aims to seek out the philosopher's alchemical stone – gold, the golden fæces made in the magical foundry of the bowels. Here Freudian and Marxist discourses are pointed up (psychoanalysis and materialism), and Lawrence develops the thinking of the Marquis de Sade and Charles Baudelaire. Ritual sodomy is historically a masculinist domain, in which male power is exercised. Connie here is the underdog; she is initiated into the male mysteries of power and defilement. The narrator emphasizes the religious transformation and catharsis that Connie undergoes (though for second wave feminists, that Connie seems to be taken by force is problematic, but Lawrence glosses over that fact). It is the same in other books where anal sex occurs (in *Women In Love* and *The Plumed Serpent*).

The anal sex act in *Lady Chatterley's Lover* takes place in Oliver Mellors' house (on the one night when Connie Chatterley stays there) – on his territory, under his control. It is the culmination of Mellors'

D.H. Lawrence: Infinite Sensual Violence

worship of Connie's body. There is an emphasis throughout the 1928 book on Connie's buttocks ("'Tha's got the nicest arse of anybody'" he tells her, 232). It is also the culmination of D.H. Lawrence's ambition – to say in a novel that people shit and piss. Mellors takes possession of Connie completely – body, shit, piss, ass and all. She becomes a sexual servant. Lawrence wanted to get to the foundation of things – in all his art. He wanted to get to the base of love, of people, of sex. Buggery was as far as he went. He used anal sex to show how deep and extraordinary and different was Connie's transformation (partly perhaps to distance *his* romantic novel from everyone else's, to demonstrate that *his* novel was 'more than' theirs, was plussing the conventional, heterosexual act). But he also introduced elements of rape, violence, and patriarchal power which were too intense for his text to handle or contain. Here, if you want to see the 'night of sensual passion' from a second wave feminist viewpoint, Lawrence's chauvinism is revealed for all to see. One can sympathize with his need to portray tenderness and transformation, but for some feminists he has chosen the wrong means – having the woman subjected to masculinist ritual and control.

Also, debates in sexual issues have moved on since the late 1920s, when Bertie Lawrence wrote the three *Lady Chatterleys*, and also from the 1960s, 1970s and 1980s, when the debates about pornography and sexual depictions were at their height. That was also the period when second wave feminism was at its most vociferous in denouncing pornography and the exploitation of women in the media and literature. Anal sex, for instance, is not the controversial issue it once was, and if *Lady Chatterley's Lover* were written today, in the 21st century, it would require some other sex act to achieve the same artistic and thematic result. (Several obvious comparisons from the 2000s and 2010s come to mind – such as the rise in women's erotica, and S/M fictions such as the *Fifty Shades of Grey* series).

One could read D.H. Lawrence's novel of sexual liberation as satire – perhaps he could be sending up patriarchy in *Lady C*, trying to show how men have buggered people for centuries, politically as well as personally. But there is no irony in the 'night of sensual passion' scene. There is little irony in any of D.H. Lawrence's sex scenes – extreme and infinite sensual violence, yes, but not much detachment or satire. He rarely stands back and views the scene from a distance, as Thomas Hardy might. He is in there, living it all with his characters (his fiction rarely makes fun of sex, for example, but takes it all seriously). We know that Lawrence really *means it.*

2

D.H. Lawrence's (Sex) Symbols

Some of the erotic symbols that David Herbert Lawrence employs include fire, peacocks, horses, the sun, water, Pan, fish and the colour red. The following is a brief survey of the symbols and use of symbolism in Lawrence's work.

Sometimes <u>fire</u> is a symbol in D.H. Lawrence's art – as when the horse-dealer's daughter is warmed back to life beside a fire in the short story *The Horse-Dealer's Daughter* (CSS, 423f) – but more often fire describes a feeling, as it is a way for Lawrence of describing some lust for life, such as when a flame flickers at the base of Oliver Mellors' spine in *Lady C*. Mellors is an advocate of 'fucking with a warm-heart', as he puts it (LCL, 215). One of the lasting images of that 1928 novel is of the forked, Pentecostal flame (quite different from T.S. Eliot's Pentecostal fire in *The Four Quartets*). In this famous quotation, Lawrence unites much of his symbolism: of flowers, fires, Christianity with sex and being:

My soul softly flaps in the little Pentecostal flame with you, like the peace of fucking. We fucked a flame into being. Even the flowers are fucked into being, between the sun and the earth. (LCL, 316)

Fire is also a destroyer, a force of violent catharsis and cleansing, as in the 'night of sensual passion' of *Lady C*, when Connie feels all her deepest shames being burnt away (258). D.H. Lawrence takes the traditional symbolic associations of fire, and extends them, developing his own symbology of fire. He is exploring, searching for the best expression-language for his concerns. So he speaks of flames flickering inside people (however, these are not new notions: souls and hearts, for instance, have often been described as being on fire – see the whole history of Catholic mysticism, for example, and the outpouring of mystics like St Teresa of Avila, St John of the Cross or Catherine of Genoa).

D.H. Lawrence's sun is dark. He speaks of a 'black sun' (again, this is not Lawrence's own idea – writers such as Julia Kristeva have employed the concept, to great effect in her book on depression and melancholy). Lawrence's sun partakes of both the light of consciousness and the darkness of the unconscious. 'The sun means a lot. It's almost the grace of God in itself', he wrote (Moore, 878). And in *Apocalypse* he claimed:

> What we lack is cosmic life, the sun in us and the moon in us. We can't get the sun in us by lying naked like pigs on a beach... We can only get the sun by a sort of worship: and the same the moon. By going forth to worship the sun, worship that is felt in the blood. (A, 24-25)

In the short story *Sun,* the sun is a lover – very male, and ithyphallic – the sun rises in the sky like phallic desire. The sun goes inside the main character, inside her breasts (CSS, 495). All the words in this part of *Sun* are of fire and heat: *flames, orange, gold, radiance.* Too much sun is cruel and painful – as in *The Plumed Serpent* (123, 131, 252). Towards the end of the novel there is a flame-like marriage (429).

More often, D.H. Lawrence goes to the opposite, and has the sun full of blackness. The sun is man, the moon is woman, as in orthodox symbolism. In Lawrence's fiction, the moon is more powerful – in *The Rainbow*, *The Overtone* and *Sons and Lovers*. The sun is essential, and always there, but it is the moon that sails in the dark night, and darkness is Lawrence's preferred realm. Most of his protagonists live in darkness: Ursula in *The Rainbow* is a typical example (and Count Dionys in *The Ladybird*). The people who can't reach the outer darkness (Anton in *The Rainbow*) are in some ways failures.

The <u>horse</u> is pure nature in motion in D.H.L.'s art – majestic but also destructive, heavy and dark. The horses are the final part of Ursula's 'crucifixion' in *The Rainbow*. After the encounter with the horses, she must re-birth herself. No one will do it for her. The horses are a catalyst. In *The Rainbow*, the horses help Ursula to rebirth her inner self. They force her transformation. In *Women In Love* the horse is associated with death and violence. Gerald tortures his mare (on one level it's a symbolic stand-in for Gudrun, just like Alec d'Urberville rides his mare in *Tess of the d'Urbervilles*).

The Lawrencean horse in *St Mawr* is a majestic animal of otherness, likened to the deity Pan, a dark god, a certain wildness. The horse lives in this, our world, yet it also lives in another (*Etruscan Places*, 208). The horse in *St Mawr* is a god (CSN, 287). It's the wildness of Britain (associated with Wales, a wild country, in its name, St Mawr [35] and in the setting of the story).

As with *Sun* or *The Escaped Cock*, *St Mawr* is one of those stories in which D.H. Lawrence is as bold as possible. He hides nothing; he is not subtle; the symbols and images are clear as he can make them. The horse is a multi-purpose symbol in Lawrence's hands which functions to embody the inner life of the characters. The horse is a magnificent stallion, "a lovely red-gold colour, and a dark, invisible fire seemed to come out of him" (285). Red is a favourite Lawrencean colour – he has red beards, red flames, red flowers, and blood in his fictions. The horse is a phallic sun-god, and when he kills someone, it is of course against an oak tree, the phallic, druidic tree of Britain (286).

The descriptions of the horse in *St Mawr* are wonderful. Here D.H.

D.H. Lawrence: Infinite Sensual Violence

Lawrence is perfectly in tune with his subject matter. He knows just what he's doing, and he does it very well. *St Mawr* is a bleak story, a search, a descent to primitive life – from London to Shropshire to Wales to New Mexico. The horse is the whole story, really. It symbolizes the main character Lou's deep yearning, her search. Men are derided.

Instead of a dark, passionate lover, Lou gets a horse. There is no narrative closure. *St Mawr* has no ending. There is Lou's famous soliloquy on wildness, but she, like Ursula Brangwen, has been spinning around the problem of restlessness, of dissatisfaction. So much of Lawrence's work is like this: static inwardly, despite the external drama having a narrative thrust, and a core of restlessness at the centre of it all. Or it's static outwardly, but in turmoil inwardly (most of the significant events and the real storytelling in Lawrence's fiction goes on inside people, in their thoughts, feelings, reactions, and experiences).

In a letter of January 9, 1924, D.H. Lawrence wrote of 'Horse-sense, Horse-laughter, Horse-passion' (Moore, 769). And in *Apocalypse,* he said: 'The horse, the horse! the symbol of surging potency and power of movement, of action, in man.' (A, 54) The Lawrencean horse is a modern version of the centaur, and of Pan.

Traditionally, the fish is a phallic, procreative symbol which swims in the unconscious oceans of the Mother Goddess. It is associated with sacrifice, god-eating and Ichthus, Christ as the Fish-God. The Lawrencean fish is a fertile, ithyphallic creature that swims in the womb of the sea, as this extract from the poem 'Fish' demonstrates:

> Who is it ejects his sperm to the naked flood?
> In the wave-mother?
> Who swims enwombed?
> Who lies with the waters of his silent passion, womb-element?
> – Fish in the waters under the earth. (CP, 335)

'The dolphin is the womb animal of the sea', wrote Tom Chetwynd (19). The dolphin in *Etruscan Places* is a similar hot phallus impregnating the cold mother sea (MM, 151). But the most extraordinary description of phallic fish occurs in the unfinished story *The Flying Fish*. If you've ever seen dolphins swimming off the bows of a ship you'll understand how joyous the experience can be, as Gethin Day discovers:

> Gethin Day watched spellbound... the strong-bodied fish heading in perfect balance of speed underneath, mingling among themselves in some strange single laughter of multiple consciousness, giving off the joy of life, sheer joy of life, togetherness in pure complete motion, many lusty-bodied fish enjoying one laugh of life, sheer togetherness, perfect as passion. "This is the most laughing joy I have ever seen, pure and unmixed... This is the purest achievement of joy I have seen in all my life: these strong, careless fish... the togetherness of love is nothing to the spinning unisons of dolphins playing under-sea." ... There as he leaned over the bowsprit he was mesmerized by one thing only, by joy, by joy of life, fish speeding in water, with playful joy. (P1, 794-5)

This is probably the happiest moment in all of D.H. Lawrence's work. Certainly it counts as a mystical experience, recalling St Teresa and St Catherine of Genoa, as well as some of the Sufi mystics (Rumi, al-Ghazzali, Jami *et al*).

The phallus is something to be worshipped in D.H. Lawrence's art. It is behind or associated with many of his symbols – horse, fire, lion, dragon, snake – but in *Lady Chatterley's Lover* it actually appears. In the flesh! Connie kneels before Mellors' penis, worshipping at its high altar. Seriously committed though he is to a phallic religion, Lawrence could not render this scene believable. Nobody could. Here the bonds between the symbolic and the real world break, and the Lawrencean edifice, painstakingly constructed, collapses into hilarity.

The erect penis is one of the more censored images in the Western world of recent times (along with images such as a naked, pregnant woman). D.H. Lawrence rightly targets it as a holy masculine secret, at the base of secular power. The penis rises out of gold-red hair, again, the Lawrencean colour of phallic, fiery power (the roots of Lawrence's modern form of phallic sexuality go back to the Ancient Roman cult of

Priapus, for example, or the use of phallic totems in prehistoric magic).

D.H. Lawrence puts everything into *Lady Chatterley's Lover*. He is out in the open, he hides nothing, and makes himself vulnerable. So he sets himself up to be shot down by anyone. Feminists have rightly sprung upon the penis-worshipping scene as an example of Lawrence's dubious sexual politics, or even his misogyny. He is at least honest, artistically, in this scene. But it can't work. It is laughable. But it is true: the erect phallus – "'So big! and so dark and so cock-sure!'" as Connie gasps (LCL, 218) – is a motif that, for second wave feminists, lies behind so much of male power and violence. Lawrence gets that right (or anticipates 1980s feminism), even if it is ridiculous.

More usual is D.H. Lawrence's exaltation of what he dubbed 'phallic consciousness'. He uses the phallus mythically, it is an object of affirmation, life and resurrection, as in Celtic, Roman and Hindu cultures (the *lingam* of Hinduism, for instance, the cosmic, phallic (Shiva) counterpart of the *yoni* of the Goddess). It is an object of joy, Lawrence noted in *Etruscan Places* (MM, 109). In 1927, he said he put a phallus into each of his paintings (Moore, 967). He speaks of phallic consciousness and 'the old phallic insouciance' (ib., 1064). In 'A Propos of *Lady Chatterley's Lover*' he commented:

> ...the phallus is only the great old symbol of godly vitality in a man, and of immediate contact. (SP, 353)

The Christian Cross is for Lawrence a phallic symbol, reaching to blood and darkness (ib., 477). More extraordinary is calling the Resurrection of Christ phallic (553). In Lawrence's theories, all these things are bound up together (British artist Eric Gill had similar ideas, however: like Lawrence, Gill sexualized Christ, drawing him with a penis, and in some drawings giving Jesus an erection. 'After all, since in his physical nature he was every inch a man, Jesus must have had proper genitals', Gill pointed out (in R. Heppenstall, 99). Gill's drawing entitled *Deposition* show the naked, dead Jesus turned towards the viewer, his genitals and pubic hair clearly visible. Gill has made Christ what some critics coyly refer to as 'well-endowed'. If Gill was going to give Christ a penis, it might as well be large (contrary to the images of Jesus in the Renaissance where, if the penis was shown at all (which was rare), it was small and unobtrusive).

Often, Eric Gill's ithyphallic imagery, like D.H. Lawrence's, can be unintentionally comical, as in Gill's engraving *God Sending* (1926), which shows Jesus flying towards the earth with an erection, his head beaming with light, with God's hand behind him, in Heaven, sending Christ on his way. Jesus's genitals are the optical centre of the composition. Here is that most blasphemous of images: not only an erotic Christ, but Christ with a erection! Gill, Fiona MacCarthy reckoned, 'felt almost proprietorial about Christ's genitals' (M, 212).

Lady Chatterley's Lover is a novel of phallic consciousness gone wild. In *The First Lady Chatterley* there is that wonderful (but also silly) line: '"the penis... connects us sensually with the planets"' (156). The penis is full of blood, mystery and life. In the second *Lady Chatterley*, the phallus is rooted in the gamekeeper's soul, it is his godhead, no less:

> ...his phallus rose in its own weird godhead, with its own swarthy pride and surety, and 'fucking' went to the phallic roots of his soul. (JTLJ, 237-8)

Enclosed in the phallic circle, like a yolk in an egg (ib., 239), Connie Chatterley becomes reborn (240), and the main point of the phallus in the Lawrencean system of erotic philosophy is for rebirth, for a new sense of touch. The point of the phallus is to be crucified and reborn. D.H. Lawrence and Connie exalt the penis, as if it were some kind of pan-cosmic god (312), but it is only one side of the relation. Lawrence exalts the phallus at the expense of the womb. Lawrence's philosophy is dualistic, and to be authentic to himself he must have light and dark, the two things, eternal opposition, a restless to and fro. So he must have the womb, too. But when he leaves out the womb, and he falls down, then he fails.

Darkness is a symbol, an atmosphere, a setting, a theme and even a belief in D.H. Lawrence's art. There are many kinds of darkness in Lawrence's work: psychological, religious, emotional, ideological. So many scenes occur at night. There is blackness in the landscape (as in *The Plumed Serpent*, 81f), and blackness in people (in Ramon, ib., 221).

During Ursula Brangwen's first kiss with Anton Skrebensky in 1916's *The Rainbow,* 'she drifted through strands of heat and darkness' (345). The rainbow-girl begins to know darkness, to descend into it. Love transforms Ursula. She becomes radiant – 'she was filled with light... Bright with an amazing light she was' (352). At the wedding, Ursula goes deeper into the darkness – the darkness of emotion inside her, and the outer darkness of unknown experiences. Ursula grows.

> Waves of delirious darkness ran through her soul. She wanted to let go... She wanted to reach and be among the flashing stars... She was mad to be gone... The darkness was passionate and breathing with immense perceived heaving. It was waiting to receive her in her flight. And how could she start – and how could she let go? She must leap from the known into the unknown. Her feet and hands beat like a madness. (363-4)

D.H. Lawrence starts to use the word darkness in all sorts of ways. It can mean the forces powering Ursula, or her ground of being, or the new experiences that love brings her, or the unknown. He writes: '[t]he darkness was passionate and breathing with an immense, unperceived heaving' (364). He is writing in the dark. He doesn't know exactly what he wants to say sometimes. Or he knows, and feels it, but can't find the right words. Often, it appears as if Lawrence is feeling his way towards what's trying to say in darkness himself. In Birkin-mode, in *Women In Love*, Lawrence notes: 'What was the good of talking, any way? It must happen beyond the sound of words.' (WL, 327) Certainly in Lawrence's art words such as *darkness, strange, being* and so on have to carry all sorts of meanings. Lawrence is forever searching, like his characters. Now he uses 'darkness', but later he might say 'being' or 'transcendence'. (And of course he keeps repeating the same words and the same phrases in slightly different combinations, as he tries to get at very abstract notions).

In *The Rainbow,* Anton Skrebensky speaks of the different darknesses in England and Africa (496), but his perceptions are far less subtle than Ursula's. She is way ahead of him. The passion that occurs is darkness melting into darkness (some of these ideas are so abstract as to be emptied of value). Dark Africa envelops her in the 'turgid, teeming night', the darkness vibrates, closes in on her (496-7). The darkness is vast – the lights of the town, of humanity, look stupid and small. In the consummation Ursula enters Paradise:

> She passed away as on a dark wind, far, far away into the pristine darkness of paradise, into the original immortality. She entered the dark fields of immortality. (502)

These are big statements, and D.H. Lawrence passionately believes in them (yet they are also delightfully speculative, a poetry of metaphysical abstractions, so abstract that passing into the dark fields of immortality can mean anything you like).

In *Women In Love,* Ursula B. touches a deeper darkness with Rupert B. The touch is deeper, and the darkness richer (402-3). Pure night surrounds them as they make love. She touches him purely, lambently, unknowingly, in pure being. It is a mystic, sensual and fulfilling consummation.

The darkness here, as in *The Ladybird* and the later fiction, is a big space within the soul. It is liberating, but also dangerous. But only in total darkness can the pure touch occur (in *The Blind Man,* for instance, as well as in *The Rainbow, The Ladybird, Women In Love,* and *The Princess*, etc). It is a touch of lower selves, a sensual not cerebral consummation (always sex in the body, not in the head, with Bertie Lawrence).

It is often connected with death. Count Dionys says in *The Ladybird*: "'In the night, in the dark, and in death, you are mine'", to Daphne, and she mutely agrees (CSN, 270). In the darkness, they shall be together. He is Lord of the Underworld (Pluto crops up in Lawrence's poems). The

D.H. Lawrence: Infinite Sensual Violence

darkness here is an eternal realm of death, connected with the blackness underlying the people and the landscape of *The Plumed Serpent.* Though more masculine than feminine, especially in middle-period Lawrence, the darkness is also associated with birth, the womb and the mother. At the end of *Sons and Lovers*, Paul Morel drifts in a vast darkness that 'outpasses' the stars and the sun. He is in a vast mother-space. He cries 'Mother!', a primal cry and the darkness helps him to be reborn, for he moves towards the lights, the lights which Ursula despises, but Paul resigns himself to.

In *The Rainbow*, Ursula Brangwen gives us the central Lawrencean image of humanity gathered around the fire of consciousness (487-8). The inner light is of science, knowledge, everyday life. Naturally Ursula looks outwards, to the wild things, to where 'the darkness wheeled about', where the angels and devils roam. Ursula is developing into an angel, a 'phallic angel' as D.H. Lawrence says in the second *Lady Chatterley* (JTLJ, 240).

In 1928's *Lady Chatterley's Lover,* darkness takes on a new role, and becomes entwined with the 'dark', shameful, secret places which the phallus hunts out. Disregarding for a moment the chauvinism (and crude dualism) at work here, the point of the sequence is rebirth. Birth-images are noted many times. Connie sleeps within the circle of the man, an egg in a cup, a yolk in an egg, her breast in the socket of his hand (JTLJ, 237-240). The outer darkness winds up being phallic. Ursula in *The Rainbow* conceives it the other way around: phallic science enclosed by the wider (and wilder) feminine outer darkness. Lawrence has swung round completely by the time of *Lady Chatterley* – the patriarchal slant of the leadership novels was still too near, too recent.

Blood-sympathy, blood-consciousness, a religion of the <u>blood</u> – this is another of D.H. Lawrence's ways of getting down to the essence of things. Most of his philosophy is based upon the body (which's partly why it was also dubious and shaky, leaning towards biologism and essentialism). In *Fantasia of the Unconscious* he starts charting the psychosexual development of the human animal with the solar plexus. He goes on to elucidate his doctrine of living blood. People are columns of blood – blood is another way of talking about the essence of people, their ground of being (in *The Plumed Serpent* [454]). Blood is the essence, the life of the body (Hux, 94), and Lawrence developed a 'religion of blood' (some cultures, such as Japan, have whole systems based upon blood types). All the time Lawrence is trying to get at the essence of a person – the very heart of them. So he speaks of blood, or the dark gods, or stars, or flames, or rainbows, or rivers – all these things are inside us.

As with the peacock or dolphin, D.H. Lawrence takes the traditional associations of the symbol and exaggerates them. Blood is the life principle, the soul, the stuff of life. Lawrence enlarges this and has rivers of blood inside people. The symbolism is the same, but exaggerated – and Lawrencified.

Sex is a mingling of two rivers of blood; after sex the blood is renewed, changed (F, 104; SP, 350). Blood is for D.H. Lawrence the individual's essence, a manifestation of their dark being (P2, 236; Poems, 474). It is usually a positive symbol, though in *Women In Love* the rabbit draws blood from Gudrun and the symbolism is of death-through-love. Gerald is associated with bad blood – as when he tortures the mare. Gudrun and Gerald mix the ritual of blood (wrongly) with death.

D.H. Lawrence uses many water symbols; he is one of the kings of water symbolism in Western literature. Generally it depicts the flow of life, or the womb of regeneration. Lakes, rivers, oceans and canals all feature prominently. Like Thomas Hardy and John Cowper Powys, Lawrence often uses quiet pools, secluded streams, slow-moving rivers and deep lakes. The horse-dealer's daughter is reborn in a wintry pool in *The Horse-Dealer's Daughter*. She comes out of a womb. The image is Arthurian, recalling the Grail-cauldron of the Welsh Goddess

Cerridwen. She nearly dies, but she has her Lancelot, her modern knight, the doctor, to save her. In *Women In Love,* the lake kills the newly-married lovers – again the feminine principle, in the figure of Diana, is present. The moon is also there, sinking in the sky. The White Moon-Goddess presides over the drowning.

In the same 1920 novel is the 'dark river of dissolution' motif (238), associated with white Aphrodite, the foam-born Goddess. In much of D.H. Lawrence's fiction, the symbols of the moon, whiteness, water, Aphrodite and death are linked together. In the 1916 prequel, *The Rainbow*, Ursula Brangwen uses moon-power to annihilate Anton Skrebensky. Ursula and Anton meet the family by the canal, and a later important scene takes place beside the dark river in the windy March night:

> Dark water flowing in silence through the big, restless night made her feel wild. (495)

This is pure D.H. Lawrence, pure, superb Lawrence. As he develops the sequence, the darkness dominates. The deeper meanings of Lawrence's use of water occurs: Lawrence describes sexual encounters using water imagery. The orgasms in his fiction are full of rippling and flowing motions (most famously in *Lady C*). Here the flood is unleashed – the mythical, Biblical Flood that killed Tom in *The Rainbow*. In the kisses of Anton and Ursula the Flood returns. Now it gives life, not death. The darkness begins to flow and envelop the lovers. The darkness is in motion. The consummation, as in *The Princess* or *The Ladybird*, occurs in total darkness, but here the people are filled with darkness. The darkness lives and moves, so Anton seems like 'living darkness' while '[s]he was all dark'. If the people are darkness and exist in darkness, and the space itself is also darkness, where does the darkness begin and the people end? Instead, the scenes become darkness moving into darkness. And Lawrence comes out with phrases such as '[d]arkness cleaving to darkness', and goes on to speak of the soft flow of his kiss... the warm, fecund flow of his kiss, that... flowed over her, covered her... they were one stream, one dark fecundity. (497)

Darkness cleaving to darkness – it's very abstract (or, is it meaningless?), but shows what a great stylist D.H. Lawrence was (one might invoke mystical texts such as the writings of Jan Ruysbroeck or Meister Eckhart here, or *The Cloud of Unknowing*). These simple words – *darkness, kiss, moon* – he has reclaimed them and put them to work to carry his own concerns. The key is the rhythm and repetition: he takes a concept, expresses it, goes back over it and re-words it, and also performs variations on it. For Lawrence's prose flows, often in torrents. Each novel is a river – *The Rainbow* is his biggest river, flowing from such a rich source (the women of Marsh Farm – the novel opens with a river, the Erewash [R, 41]), gathering momentum, flooding and ending up at the sea. (Hence also the form of Lawrence's poetry, which, like Walt Whitman's, employed very long lines, an overlapping, flowing kind of poesie).

The <u>moon</u> and the <u>sea</u> – D.H. Lawrence couldn't have conjured up two richer or more powerful symbols for the matchless, ecstatic scene in *The Rainbow* where Ursula cries out, "'I want to go!'". There are no more powerful symbols. The rainbow symbol is majestic, and it connects up, in its arching movement, the themes of the novel. But it is the moon and the ocean which represent Ursula's apotheosis, her beatification and martyrdom.

The moon and the ocean appear in *Sons and Lovers* when Paul Morel and Miriam are by the sea after looking at a rainbow image – the Norman arches of the church (SL, 229). Water, blood, the arch, the moon, flames, darkness and kisses are all noted in this lyrical scene, all on one page (it's true, too, that D.H. Lawrence's (sex) symbols, wonderfully deployed as they are, do become somewhat interchangeable, and the moon can perform a similar function to water or blood or a rainbow). A deathly white moon over the sea appears in *Kangaroo* when Somers has a vision of the Goddess. The night is full of the seething water, 'heaving like a woman with unspeakable desire' (K, 375. 'Unspeakable' maybe – but that doesn't stop Lawrence trying to speak it and write about it). Here Lawrence's narrator reacts against the Goddess. The narrator is terrified of the Goddess in motion – the night, the whiteness, the moon, the violent ocean – all the traditional motifs of the Goddess since earliest times repel Somers, and *Kangaroo*'s narrator. The feminine principle is too strong, too deep and too out of control for him, just as Ursula Brangwen is too big and too extravagant for Anton Skrebensky. Anton takes Ursula into the darkness, down by the sea, on vacation, but he can't handle her.

Paul Morel drags Clara Dawes to the swollen River Trent to find a place to make love in *Sons and Lovers*. They get trapped by the river (SL, 374). Again, the male gets out of his depth in the oceanic female. Joey the peacock floundering in the snow in *Wintry Peacock*, Gerald in the snow in *Women In Love*, Anton by the sea in *The Rainbow*, Paul by the river in *Sons and Lovers*, Birkin by the lake in *Women In Love* – all of these are images of the male character being swamped by the larger feminine principle. Birkin tries to shatter the moon and water by force, tries to overcome it as Anton could not. But his fight is rather pathetic. And when the Goddess (Ursula) appears at the lake, his ineffectuality is pointed out, and painfully. Birkin, in fact, reveals a rather brutal chauvinism from time to time. For instance, he talks about the Goddess's desire for 'unspeakable intimacies' (*Women In Love*, 343). Something about women repulses him.

This situation is reversed in the novel *The Plumed Serpent:* Kate, the heroine, sails on a sperm-like lake. The male adrift on a feminine sea is a common image in world literature (in *The Odyssey*, or *Moby Dick*), but the opposite is unusual. The lake of sperm is depicted here as lifeless (on its own), and the general atmosphere of the chapter "The Lake" in *The Plumed Serpent* is one of vacuity and emptiness. Kate is sailing into a masculine world of dry thunder and ideological violence.

More joyous is the scene in *Lady Chatterley's Lover* where Connie Chatterley runs naked in the rain (230). Water is a female domain.

Oliver Mellors doesn't like the rain (well, *duh,* no one in Britain does!). Though D.H. Lawrence admits the sea is a womb – in *Etruscan Places* (150) – it is forever associated with death. The ocean, which is life on so many levels, is death in Lawrence's art. The ocean-womb is death. Lawrence is very reactionary/ masculinist in this respect, re-stating the ancient connections between Hell, death and the womb (and the vagina as the Mouth of Hell). It's all paranoia, a manifestation of men's fear of women, Jungian projection, literal demonization, as feminists have often pointed out. The Lawrencean male character dives down into the oceanic womb occasionally – Mellors tups Connie in the rain, has his orgasm, then dashes back to his hut. Similarly, in *Etruscan Places,* Lawrence remarks of the dolphin, a symbol of the Christ-Man-Phallus type:

> He [the dolphin] is so much alive, he is like the phallus carrying the fiery spark of procreation down into the wet darkness of the womb. The diver does the same, carrying like a phallus his small hot spark into the deeps of death (MM, 151)

All of these symbols and considerations become a bit boring after a while – a bit limited. Could D.H. Lawrence go no further? Half the time he seems to be using his (sex) symbolism in such an obvious, non-subtle way. His symbols are one-sided all too often, such as the flood in *The Virgin and the Gipsy,* which is so clichéd – complete with stampeding horses (a variation on the ending of *The Rainbow*). But Lawrence's fiction is also entirely metaphorical, abstract, and symbolic – and if you take it out you extract the beating heart of it. Lawrence simply thinks and writes in terms of symbols and mythology. He can't help being poetic (musical, rhythmic, repetitive), it's his default position as an author (like his massive over-writing, his hundred slightly different ways of saying the same thing).

No matter how often D.H. Lawrence uses a symbol like water or the moon, he will always come back to them. He never tires of them (like the troubadours with symbols such as fire, hearts, flowers and love, or the Romantics with oceans, infinity and night). But there is also a point where the uses of a symbol run out, and Lawrence's prose reaches a ceiling of psychological value, and can rise (or sink) no further.

3

Infinite Sensual Violence

The Rainbow

The Rainbow (1916) is one of the greatest novels ever written. No question about that. It has such weight, such poetic density. You recognise this as soon as you pick it up. Dip into it anywhere. Every sentence throbs with such poetic energy. It is a really remarkable book. This is the first thing you can say about it.

We enter the world of D.H. Lawrence's *The Rainbow* as if entering a Cathedral, a vast and familiar space still fresh with new wonders. Lawrence shows that the wonders are right here, right inside us, and beside us, and around us, even in mundane places such as the North Midlands, around Nottingham, even in the quite ordinary back streets and houses of boring, old, provincial England. These are the 'sequestered spots' of Thomas Hardy's Wessexscape, those out-of-the-way places that to the outsider seem harmless and mundane enough, yet which can contain truly great tragedies of a Sophoclean grandeur.

Big stuff, and it's all right here, right inside us and around us. The pulse of passion is there, according to Lorenzo – you have to know is how to bring it out, to tease it out into the open. Few writers could do this as well as D.H.L. when he was on form, and in *The Rainbow*, Lawrence is as on form as he ever was.

D.H. Lawrence begins his classic novel of the Brangwens at full throttle, writing as densely and as passionately as he ever could. The opening is as full-blown as the start of Thomas Hardy's last novel, *Jude the Obscure,* although the themes are announced more stridently.

The timeline of *The Rainbow* (in the Penguin edition, edited by John Worthern), has the novel set from about 1868 to 1905. Lydia was born in 1834; Tom was born in 1840; Anna is a Lensky, Lydia's daughter (b. 1864); Will is a Brangwen, Tom's son (b. 1862); Ursula is the daughter of Anna and Will (born in 1883).

The church is the spiritual zone, the manifestation of the 'Beyond'. It stands upright on the flat earth. Female earth, supine, with the male structure, vertical – the old symbolism's still prevalent. The tower connects people to the stars, the cosmos, the ultimate 'Beyond'. The man bends back down to his work in the fields, just as in the paintings of paintings by Jean-François Millet (such as *The Gleaners*, 1857). In the first paragraph alone of *The Rainbow,* D.H. Lawrence's narrator sets up the tensions between place and work, between village and church, between the pagan, rural life and the otherworldliness of organized religion, between workers and their leaders, between nature and humanity.

The narrator is interested in livingness, in what life is, in how valuable it is. The levels in the text of ideology, politics, sexuality, ontology, religion, work and marriage are D.H. Lawrence's concerns (but he never loses sight, too, of bodies and skin and limbs and most of all, the rich, restless inner life). He describes the people's circumstances, the land's richness, and the locals' status. He weaves in his religious language soon enough, in the fifth paragraph: 'But heaven and earth was teeming around them' (41).

D.H. Lawrence: Infinite Sensual Violence

Bertie Lawrence describes the nature mysticism of the people in simple, archaic, classically pastoral terms: 'They felt the rush of the sap in spring', etc (42). Birth and life and death, the eternal cycle of the seasons, of life itself, is pointed out. The plant must die to give life to the seed. The whole 1916 novel is about birth, and the many deaths necessary for a sense of wholeness to be established. Rain, birds' nests, crops, cattle, milk – the whole pulse of life in the blood is described. Archetypal Lawrencean imagery of the birds in Fall and Winter occurs next, culminating in the quiescence of the men watching themselves besides their fires.

Then come the women.

Look at D.H. Lawrence's so-simple style: 'The women were different.' (42) No messing about there: just a plain statement, the authorial control set at full power. *The women were different.* The whole of the saga of the sisters, the two novels *The Rainbow* and 1920's *Women In Love*, pivots around this statement: *the women were different.* At the end of *The Rainbow*, Ursula Brangwen is the big yearner. At the end of *Women In Love*, the roles are reversed: the man turns out to be the big yearner for Something More Than This:

> "You are all women to me" [Birkin tells Ursula] "But I wanted a man, as eternal as you and I are eternal." (WL, 583)

The extra dimension becomes necessary for the man. It is not just the triangle of man-woman-earth anymore. Man needs another man, a different kind of mirror for his well-being. Man must have the male brotherhood.

Tom Brangwen, the first male in this Lawrencean Brangwensaga, orbited around the women, but the women looked out, to 'the wonder of the beyond'. D.H. Lawrence everywhere stresses the difference, cultural and biological, of gender (partly for dramatic effect). At the end of the 1916-20 saga, the woman turns inward, to her lover. He, meanwhile, remains unsatisfied. He must still look out.

•

Back we go to the beginning of the two novels, when the man in the fields looked up to the church tower. It is the man, ultimately, that looks up and out, to the eternal Beyond of the spirit, the stars, the cosmos and the Godhead. Women look inward for the Beyond. They realize that the greatest challenges, the greatest distances, the greatest yearnings, occur on the inside, in the body and the soul. The individual, not the mass, is the site of the great religious challenges. Culture begins and ends, as Weston La Barre has demonstrated in *The Ghost Dance, in people* (1972). The big changes must occur first (and only perhaps) in people. Get people right and the rest follows – this is the basic idea. It is the mission of Lawrence's art, from *The White Peacock* to *The Escaped Cock*. As Robert Keily writes in "Accident And Purpose: "Bad Form" in Lawrence's Fiction":

> There are mining accidents in *Sons and Lovers* and floods in *The Rainbow*, but when lightning strikes a Lawrence character, it is much more likely to strike from within. Obsessive, violent, or ecstatic passion well up inside his characters, causing unexpected behavior. When external nature seems to duplicate their internal state, the effect is not really that of the pathetic fallacy, a cosmic echo, but rather a blurring of the boundaries between the individual and the world. (102)

D.H. Lawrence's fiction is founded upon this psycho-religious disruption, where the continuity between self and world, between life and death, between love and sexuality, is broken. It not merely shattered, it is irreparable.

In the two Sister Brangwen novels, D.H. Lawrence shows women to be the adventurous ones, contrary to some accepted Western beliefs. Men are traditionally the adventurers and hunters: they go *out*, the women stay in and mind the house and children, in the conventional view of gender roles. But the men's 'out' is really escape – to escape the house and family, to the otherness that for Lawrence is symbolized by the other male, the man-friend. Man goes 'out', but his 'out' is conservative, static, working in the fields. He comes back and vegetates in front of the fire, an image still seen in contemporary life – the man of the house sitting in the armchair with his pipe, slippers and newspapers (1930-1960s), or on the couch watching sport on TV (1950s-now). He comes in from 'outside', but is in fact ultimately passive. Meanwhile, the woman is doing all the work in the house. Measured financially, as paid-labour, the woman does twice as much work, if not more than the man (as feminists have pointed out). Hence the woman's dissatisfaction. She wants Something More Than This. *Is this all?* asks the woman. There *must* be more than this!

There is. There is more – the 'spoken world' for a start, which D.H. Lawrence disliked but without which Western society would collapse. In *The Rainbow*, there is the road, the village, the church, the world beyond. The Beyond is a yearned-for goal, the object of many nomadic journeys. The women face outwards. They *yearn*. They want to be in the thick of things, where real life goes on. Things happening – they want mythologies, for myths tells us *what is happening.* The global media machine has taken over this function. It seems to tell us what is happening. It bestows meanings upon the world's events (but only some of them, and only in a very narrow manner). In the same way, the local women in *The Rainbow* live through the life of Mrs Hardy in her manor house just as audiences of soap operas live through TV characters. Soap operas give people a fictional version of the sense of community they think they've lost (but which never existed in the first place). The global media is not spiritual, but worldly, and in *The Rainbow* the women crave secular involvement. They want to be part of the world. They desire *to know*. The vicar becomes the community's shaman – the one 'who spoke the other, magic language' (43).

Their men are so ordinary. Woman want magic, heightened realities, deeper meanings, richer lives. The vicar, disseminating the tired rhetoric of his near-dead, desert religion, at least seems a little magical – anything is more magical to the women than this lazy sitting by the fire. It's the women in D.H. Lawrence's art who cry like Samuel Beckett's derelicts in *Waiting For Godot*: "Nothing happens!" It's an eternal cry, this anguished dissatisfaction with life. It must be as old as humankind. There're always things to do, but still 'nothing happens'. How fresh and contemporary Lawrence is, finding in the female characters an anxious restlessness, a great yearning. We can see the worldwide media now fulfilling such yearnings with materialist gratifications of unspoken yearnings – soap operas, movies, magazines, blockbuster novels, advertizing, TV commercials, mass consumption – all full of fantasies of things happening, of life being lived, somewhere else. The eternal fantasy of advanced capitalist societies, the tease, the promise, the come-on that can never be fulfilled (desire breeds more desire, as the feminist philosopher Elizabeth Grosz put it).

Thus Ursula and Anna and Lydia (the three generations of women in *The Rainbow*), push their men forward, onto better things. There's got to be something better than this, the women cry, so they push their men onward and outward, to find it. They force their men to re-examine their roles as hunter-gatherers – as hunters of the life paradisal, which must lie in the future, not in some past Golden Age. Restlessness, not nostalgia, desire not gratification. The Great Yearning continues to push people along.

So much yearning, and this is the dynamic of *The Rainbow*, culminating in the figure of Ursula Brangwen, who is all question and need and desire and dissatisfaction. D.H. Lawrence is equivocal – the women push their men out and partly bring about their own destruction. Thus the goal is self-responsibility, not self-immolation. The achievement of one's self.

Marriage is the battleground. In *The Rainbow*, the spoken world, the exhausted religion signified by the church and the vicarage, the life lived through the upper classes, knowledge, freedom, work and the Beyond – all these are fought for within the boundaries of Western marriage. Marriage, for Bertie Lawrence, means the relation of man and woman, the big Lawrencean theme, the relation that must encompass and satisfy every level of existence: the spiritual, sensual, ideological, political, physical and historical. The woman wants to get everything right: work, love, sex, money, house, children, parenthood, art –

all these must blossom, not just trundle along. Painfully for the man, the woman makes all of this conscious. She brings all of these concerns into the light. The man cannot bear to look at some of them. What does it matter? he thinks. Let them alone. But no, a new restlessness among the women is in the air, and in their bodies. They will *not* let well alone. They will disturb the world until it is analyzed and put right. A big ambition, and near-impossible to achieve, perhaps. But the man who doesn't try is, in the woman's eyes, worse than lazy, he's dead. To be alive is to be engaged in the fight. Someone not in the thick of things, who prefers to work robotically in the fields (or the office), and who flops in front of the fire (these days the TV or internet or cel phone), is dead, a non-man, a non-human being. This is one of D.H. Lawrence's major concerns, and we find it in much of his work, right up to the last essays.

Women look to the outside: Lydia comes from the outside, and Anna. Ursula is half an outsider, a mixture of Brangwen and Polish. The tensions in her character are ethnic as well as sociological, environmental, religious, and ontological.

※

The Earth is a Goddess – in *The Rainbow*'s very first paragraph – the flat Earth upon which men work and build their religions. As the narrative unfolds it turns out that Lydia becomes a typical Lawrencean Goddess of Flowers.

Flowers form a large part of the *mise-en-scene* and symbolism of D.H. Lawrence's work – particularly in *Lady Chatterley's Lover, The White Peacock* and *Sons and Lovers*. Lydia is associated with many flowers, as Lawrence describes her inner moods. As her soul is roused, she begins to know the mysteries of primroses, bluebells, heather, gorse and snowdrops. Out of the push and flow of life, Lawrence pulls one or two flowers to crystallize the emotions of his characters and to add to the meanings of the story. Thus from the room of the dying vicar in Yorkshire, Lydia stares at the snowdrops. Battered by the wind, they still cling to the Earth, are not blown away (90).

D.H. Lawrence: Infinite Sensual Violence

In the courtship scene in *The Rainbow*, one of those 'ritual scenes' (magical scenes is a better term) in which time is frozen and the moment is pregnant with significance, Tom Brangwen brings a bunch of daffodils, the Easter lily. Again, as in the death scene at the rectory, the wind is blowing noisily and powerfully. Tom looks in through the window, as Aaron does in *Aaron's Rod*. It is one of those frozen moments which D.H. Lawrence is so good at evoking. Lydia is again a Goddess-figure, this time a Western Madonna and Child, framed by the window, as in many a Renaissance painting. Everything stops except for the booming wind and the singing inside. Outside is the restless energy of the air (air, breath and wind are masculine energies of phallic spirit in traditional symbolism), inside is the apparent calm of domesticity, of the mother–child relation, eternal, soft embrace. It's an illusion. There is no stasis – the wind's blowing, the clouds are moving, the moon spins through space; inside the child's attention wanders – there are things to do, all sorts of chores.

When the man enters, D.H. Lawrence's narrator shows how he disturbs the domestic equilibrium. Then the elemental stasis returns, but not after a struggle. It is an extraordinary sequence, when Lydia and Tom are sitting there in silence, while the wind roars outside. It is the first scene in the 1916 book where Lawrence winds up his passionate prose. He turns on the magic here, in this first scene of rebirth:

> He returned gradually, but newly created, as after a gestation, a new birth, in the womb of darkness. Aerial and light everything was, new as a morning, fresh and newly-begun. Like a dawn blazed in them, their new life came to pass, it was beyond all conceiving good... (81)

The end of the chapter is marvellous, with the wind blowing gaping holes in the big night – a superb image of Tom's new, bewildered state. Not much's happening, in terms of story and events, it's mainly psychological (as often in Lawrence's fiction, where events are all internal – mental states, views, feelings).

In 1922's *Aaron's Rod*, the man again looks in from the darkness.

The tension is the opposite of *The Rainbow* sequence, for here Aaron finds domestic life hideous – all those houses squashed in together, everyone living on top of each other, recalling André Gide's pronouncement: 'Families, I hate you' (AR, 52). Marriage, which was a mystery, becomes a misery (56).

In *Sons and Lovers,* it is the woman who is thrust out into the night. But in this role-reversal, it is the woman outside who enjoys a moon-soaked glorification. Mrs Morel is apotheosized as a latter-day Virgin Mary, complete with moon, lilies and a shining whiteness. While Mr Morel sinks into stupor, she radiates among the white lilies and white roses.

Eugene Goodheart describes the scene where Tom and Lydia make love for the first time in *The Rainbow* in his study *Desire and Its Discontents*:

> The setting is a dark, virtually invisible space in which the lovers are swept by a passion felt in the breasts and the bowels. The language describing the scene is the language of suffering. It is a kind of religious passion, a dissolution of an old self and the birth of a new. The stages are the familiar ones of suffering, sleep, and reawakening or rebirth. These are demanding conditions, an extraordinary burden for the sexual act. One might read the scene as a religious event, a scene of fulfilment. And certainly in later scenes, their coming together occurs in a transcendent realm, a divine space, inaccessible to ordinary lovers. (63-64)

Another sacramental scene that involves cold, outer darkness and inner warmth and light in *The Rainbow* is when Tom carries Anna into the barn. The silent, wondering child and the man holding her in a trance in the 'timeless stillness' (116), is such a stunning scene. D.H. Lawrence uses the simplest language, the simplest of images – a man and a girl in a barn on a rainy night. Yet he is wondrous. He shows a very positive image of patriarchy – the father-figure as solid and dependable, knowing exactly what to do and so caring. Yet he holds a future Goddess in his arms, a woman who will dance naked, fully pregnant, annihilating her man.

Such yearning in D.H. Lawrence's art. *The Rainbow* flows so well from one ritual, magical moment to the next.

After the barn sequence there is the gorgeous evocation of the childhood of Anna Lensky. What a fierce little creature she is, with her dancing and skipping and wild ways. D.H. Lawrence is so accurate here as he describes Anna sitting beside Tom on the trap (with a horse) going to market. He really captures some of the exuberance of youth here. There is another magic time when Tom and Lydia make love again, after so long. Tom feels trapped. Like Will later on, he wants to smash down the walls, to let the night in (129). When he and Lydia dissolve into each other it is a transfiguration, it is a religious transformation (133). Tom is placated. Stillness returns. Sacred time is re-instated. Tom bows down before the Goddess – 'She was now the transfigured, she was wonderful, beyond him... Easiest he could kiss her feet' (132). In the same way mediæval saints prostrated themselves before the Virgin Mary, and troubadours before their beloveds.

There is always something dark in Lydia, something remote and secret and to do with her past that Tom Brangwen cannot touch. Their love-making is religious; they move out; they expand; they move into a new, bigger, mythic sense of space. This glorification is a birth, a rebirth, just as Tom was reborn when he met Lydia for the first time. The 1916 book is a series of rebirths, and it takes all kinds of shocks to knock the self into self-realization. Transformation is painful, and from Tom, through Anna to Ursula, it gets more and more pain-stricken.

※

For the moment, the rainbow is mended. It spans again between Heaven and Earth, between men and women. Deep connections have been made – for a while. But it doesn't last and Tom Brangwen soon becomes restless again. After puberty, Anna begins to madden him. He can't handle adulthood, people becoming mature. He is the spirit of patriarchy, the man of the earth, of blood, sweat, tears and toil. He embodies conservative, reactionary masculinity, disliking change, uncertainty, anything new. He is locked in the blood-intimacy, and caught deep in the thrall of the Goddess. As Anna becomes a Goddess she rises above him. Lydia stands in the wings, indifferent, as Anna rises above Tom, to become a deity.

The new man, Will, is a harder version of Tom. He is more stubborn, more steel-like. Anna is strong. She doesn't yet, unlike Tom, realize her limitations. She still regards him as pure patriarchy – he is for her 'a kind of Godhead, he embraced all manhood for her' (144). But slowly Anna's emotions slip from her father to her lover, just as for Tom the beloved replaced his mother and sister. In *Sons and Lovers,* D.H. Lawrence spends a long time recreating this psychic sea-change, the displacement and replacement, this œdipal shift of allegiances. He is much faster in *The Rainbow*.

Religion is the world in which Anna Lensky meets Will Brangwen in *The Rainbow*. Her religious feelings are diffuse – she feels a strange passion on repeating the *Ave Maria* (pp. 141-2). Will crystallizes some of her feelings. Their first major meeting is in the church (of course). It is the laughter of God that joins them. In another magical scene, Anna has hysterics at Will's singing, and '[h]er soul opened in amazement', comments D.H. Lawrence (148). She wakes up to another person, someone separate from her father (and herself): another man.

The whole scene is bathed in laughter, as well as the 'illumination and luminous shadow all around her' (147). As in classic fiction, the exterior glow of the stained glass reflects Anna's inner state. But D.H. Lawrence describes people's emotional states in a way that connects up the exterior, churchy *mise-en-scene* with an interior, spiritual state. He mixes in the narrative discourse and the religious, ideological discourse simultaneously. All writers, all art does this, but Lawrence does it with a deeper power than almost any other writer. It is his special gift, this magical blending of the exterior and the interior, the plot and the theme.

The magical binder is his *language,* his way of fusing together words, quite ordinary words, but in a way that is deep. D.H. Lawrence seems to be writing at rock bottom, at the very centre of life, at the base of the human psyche, the seat of the soul, what the mystics called the 'Ground of Being'. Lawrence aims for the mystics' 'Divine Ground'. Lawrence, when he's writing about Anna and Will in the church, Anna and Will singing, he evokes the core of life. His narrator persona is there, in the midst of life. At his best, he is writing life, just as the *Bible* writes life, creates it, or William Shakespeare or Dante Alighieri write life. Where writing and life (and reading) become part of the same thing. Like Will, Lawrence is touched by the Hand of God. His book is the 'bright book of life', his term for what the novel could be. Bright as stained glass, glowing with the sun behind it. It all seems very real to us. Not dreamlike, but tactile, right there in the thick of things. No mediation, just the real life, right in front of us. Lawrence's art is unified – it burns, and here in *The Rainbow* and in a few other places (*The Escaped Cock, St Mawr, Lady Chatterley's Lover, Women In Love,* and *Sons and Lovers*), it burns into one solid, monumental artform.

Anna opens up her soul to Will, just as we must open up our souls to D.H. Lawrence and his 1916 book. He throws everything he's got into *The Rainbow,* which is why so much burns out of it. The fire is deep within his work, and the flames lick us just as they lick his characters.

Do away with edging around the metaphor. Not 'Anna is like a flame', but 'Anna is a flame'. Similarly, reading is not *like* having a rebirth, it *is* a rebirth.

The rebirth is manifold – for the characters, for D.H. Lawrence, for us. He takes us into the beyond. We go through the pain with the characters – the 'wonder and birthpain of love' (162).

So the 1916 novel is religious because it is about rebirth, about the individual becoming self-responsible, about the re-instatement of a sacred, mythic time, about finding and returning to the centre.

All these religious and ontological themes are pushed into the foreground by Anna and Will and the church. It is a grey, Protestant church from which the Goddess (the Virgin Mary) has been thrown out (in the political separation of Britain from Catholicism). But it is still a

D.H. Lawrence: Infinite Sensual Violence

church which is a great womb, has a womb-like darkness inside it. When you enter a church you enter the Goddess, as Joseph Campbell put it, you enter the womb, the womb of the Goddess, you move back into a primal, sacred time and space. The centre is regained, time is abolished and female space becomes everything.

When Anna and Will go into the church in *The Rainbow* they seem (externally) to enter a masculinist territory, associated with the mystic Lamb, the Hand of God in Will's sculpture (so much like an idea from the art of Auguste Rodin and Eric Gill), and that opening paragraph, when the men looked up from the field to see the spire. In fact, they return to a feminine space, which even hundreds of years of stern, patriarchal Anglicized Christianity cannot erase. The church is feminine, and inside it the woman is more powerful than the man. Will sings, but Anna laughs, and it is the laughter of power. However well he sings, she laughs louder. He might be carried away by church architecture (150-1), but she is carried further, and deeper. She is the more powerful one. She controls the relationship. This is shown so clearly in the magnificent cornfield scene, one of the most erotic scenes in world literature.

※

The cornfield scene is pure sex really, pure sex in literature.

Everything here is erotic – the language, the rhythm, the repetition, the imagery, the setting, the point in the story, the *mise-en-scene*, the look of the characters, their voices, and the goal of the whole sequence. It's one of the scenes that renders D.H. Lawrence so memorable. I can read this piece again and again. It's so rich.

Anna has already embraced him and moaned, "'Will, I love you, I love you, Will, I love you'" (156). This sequence, at night, in the farmyard buildings, in August, in the rain, is the simple mirror of the earlier barn scene when Tom carried Anna out to calm her. Now she is grown – a Goddess in the making.

She is dancing away from her father Tom, making the mythic, œdipal movement from father to lover. The father watches, powerless, seething. He sees the lovers embracing against the light – the image comes straight out of Thomas Hardy's fiction: the impotent voyeur and the loving couple.

The setting of the cornfield is pregnant with symbolism. Associated with gods, with Christ, the Eucharist, with phallicism and bounty, corn is the emblem of Goddesses such as Demeter, Isis, Artemis, Cybele and Virgo, the Virgin. It is found in Ancient Egyptian, Chinese, Persian, Mediterranean rituals. Much of J.G. Frazer's *The Golden Bough* is devoted to corn rites. Lorenzo was aware of all this and instead of keeping it in the background, he thrusts the religious symbolism forward. Anna is a Virgin Corn-Goddess, a latter-day Ishtar meeting her doomed lover, Tammuz. The moon, *the* symbol prime of the Goddess in all her manifestations, presides over the field. The scene thus has as much symbolism as any ritual in the West. Lawrence explicitly references the opening paragraph too – the shocks stand erect on the open field, phallic, like little people, like the church tower in the second sentence of the novel.

D.H. Lawrence is so bold in this scene in *The Rainbow*, so romantic, so weighty in his symbolism and discourse, yet he comes through. It is one of his finest pieces of writing. He's working at full power. With all the precision of the most meticulous painter he sets the scene: the moon, the girl, the boy, the field. It's stark but also lush. The rhythm starts up. It is the push-me-pull-you rhythm of lovemaking. There is sharpness, hissing, weight, closeness, effort – all the imagery of sex. Things glisten, the moon throbs in Anna's bosom. She opens to the great mysteries of life. Love and work, sex and politics are fused, and transcended. The beyond opens to them. She lets him possess her physically, but she towers over him spiritually. She has all the moon's power inside her. It's beaming down into her. She absorbs the moon. Like Ursula, she can annihilate her man with moon-power, with the magic of the Goddess. When they embrace, it's as good as any love-scene in literature – as good as Francesco Petrarch, Ovid, Emily Brontë:

Trembling with keen triumph, his heart was white as a star as he drove his kisses nearer.

"My love!" she called, in a low voice, from afar. The low sound seemed to call to him from far off, under the moon, to him who was unaware. He stopped, quivered, and listened.

"My love," came again the low, plaintive call, like a bird unseen in the night.

He was afraid. His heart quivered and broke. He was stopped.

"Anna," he said, as if he answered her from a distance, unsure.

"My love."

And he drew near, and she drew near.

"Anna," he said, in wonder and birthpain of love.

"My love," she said, her voice growing rapturous. And they kissed on the mouth, in rapture and surprise, long. And again they were kissing together. Till something happened in him, he was strange. He wanted her. He wanted her exceedingly. She was something new. They stood there folded, suspended in the night. (162)

Simple words – *night, kiss, moonlight, wonder, quiver.* It's the music, the rhythm and repetition that gives the passage its formal magic. But D.H. Lawrence has led us up to this so carefully. He unleashes the full force of his poetic fire here. Masterful, because the woman is Mistress. Mythical because love transcends relationship. Magical because language is Queen. Mystical because beyond all is the moon and life, the Ultimate Other.

(Re-reading the Anna and Will cornfield passage in *The Rainbow* decades later, it does expose itself to the possibility of ridicule, as with D.H.L.'s hyper-lyrical prose in *Lady Chatterley*. It's super-romantic writing about something super-romantic – the kisses and embraces of lovers by moonlight in the fields. That's what readers, including myself, respond to (I can see I went particularly crazy over this passage when I first wrote this book). Thus, Lawrence makes himself vulnerable to satire.

Anyway, it's writing that you have to surrender yourself to – there's no point standing back, arms crossed, looking grumpy and sarcastically muttering, 'this is rubbish'. Maybe it *is* rubbish, but it's very high quality rubbish.

It's like dancing at a disco or a concert – you can stand and watch, immobile, critical, ironic, and, wow, you look *so cool* just standing there... or you can surrender yourself to it, and move, and dance. Music, like literature, is so much better and much more fun if you give yourself to it).

※

Matriarchy is sweeping in: Lydia over Tom, Anna over Will, Ursula over Anton. When women become self-responsible in *The Rainbow*, they are majestic. Patriarchy is fading – Tom loses his grip on things. Significantly, Anna's wedding is described from the patriarch's point-of-view. Tom dissolves into the dark blue of the window in the church. He is already partly gone. Anna is already victorious. Will is no substitute for the father-figure, Tom feels. But so tenderly D.H. Lawrence describes the age-old psychic displacement of the parent, the suddenness of old age, the rage, the impotence (and the impotent jealousy). It is as it has always been – as in the *Bible*. Matriarchy blossoms, but the patriarchal ways die hard. Anna in ascension, Tom in decline – Lawrence describes these movements so gently, yet so fiercely. He is re-writing the *Bible*, re-interpreting the *Bible*. His novel is a 'bright book of life'.

Life is and always was anxious.

The way that D.H. Lawrence's characters deal with it is a lot more authentic than the violent methods of the *Old Testament*. Lawrence's New *New Testament* tries to re-instate women/ women's agency. He's bound to fail, but the gesture is big, rich and spacious. Patriarchy must die. The old ways must die. To be reborn you must first die – to yourself, your social environment, your society, your culture. The way forward is into the unknown – the ultimate, terrifying journey. Lawrence follows Christ – and goes beyond him, rewriting the last book of the *Bible* as his own astonishing set of *Revelations*.

Incredible passion in the story of Anna and Will in *The Rainbow*. If the cornfield was a great scene, D.H. Lawrence goes even better when Anna dances pregnant. She is inside the womb/ room; the fire is hot;

she is hot with life:

> Big with child as she was, she danced there in the bedroom by herself, lifting her hands and her body to the Unseen, to the unseen Creator who had chosen her, to Whom she belonged. (224)

Anna is so powerful here. She is a Goddess now, at the height of her powers as a woman. The image alone is so powerful – the naked, pregnant, dancing woman but the symbolism, the ideology, the religious dimension is even greater, and even deeper. She is a full-blown Goddess, utterly powerful. She is big with child, big with life. This is also why a pregnant woman is one of the most often censored images in the world. Patriarchal society recognizes this power. They try to hide it, to hide from it. Wendy O'Flaherty, writing of the powerful Goddess in Hindu mythology in *Women, Androgynes, and Other Mythical Beasts*, says:

> the challenge to survive the threat of the goddess is, therefore, far more than the challenge to surmount the threat to sexual integrity: it is the challenge to survive and to grow. (87)

Will just cowers when he sees Anna dancing in the firelight. She dances to God. She opens up to God, to the beyond, to the unseen. She takes it all inside her – she is so big she can accommodate the vastness of the beyond. Such richness in Anna fully pregnant. 'The blaze of light on her heart was too beautiful and dazzling, from the conception in her womb. She walked glorified.' (220) The cornfield embrace has come to fruition, and Anna is 'like a full ear of corn.' (225).

※

Nobody's happy in *The Rainbow*, even tho' there are numerous moments of ecstasy. Re-reading the novel again, it's striking just how neurotic, paranoid and vulnerable the characters are. They are too sensitive to every tiny slight, every teensy knock that life throws at them. Underneath fester grudges, resentments, impotencies, jealousies. Nothing is right for long, something always upsets their mental equilibrium.

The Rainbow is a manic depressive text, a story of passive-aggressive manipulation, where every character is jittery, at odds with themselves, with the people around them, and with the world itself. Lorenzo can write anxiety as skilfully as any novelist.

※

There's such a depth of suffering in the Will–Anna marriage. Opened-up now, after the wedding, their relationship deepens into pain. Will is reborn – 'suddenly, like a chestnut falling out of a burr, he was shed naked and glistening on to a soft, fecund earth' (185). This is a marvellous image, capturing so sensuously Will's new birth into Mother Earth. In the chapter "Anna Victrix", they move from eternal intimacy to hateful separateness.

First they stay in bed all day. They're back in the womb. Marriage begins, at least, as a rebirth. The house is a womb, an Ark (187). Society is the Flood, and nothing can stop it. The Flood will later claim Tom – patriarchy claiming its adherents. For a while the socio-political flood is halted, but '[t]he world *was* there, after all' (187).

Religion is the battleground. Will B. wants 'the emotion of all the great mysteries of passion' from the church (199). Anna L. resents all this. The snow falls to shut them in again, but the seed of doubt has already been sown – Will has fallen onto fecund earth. Anna, the Earth-Goddess, will swallow him whole, but she will only rebirth a part of him. He will be delivered by her, become a husband (232), but at great cost (D.H. Lawrence is especially adept at evoking the costs to the soul and the psyche in a relationship, at depicting what people give up, what they lose, what they don't realize they've lost until it's too late).

Anna and Will are at odds, at opposites. She sees a lamb, he sees the Mystic Lamb of God (200). But things are always swapping around, and she becomes bigger and more universal than him. He turns into a hawk, but she too is a hawk (203) – echoes of the *Mabinogion* and the shape-changing Goddess Cerridwen. They tear each other apart when they make love. Will finds solace in the æsthetics of the church – John

Ruskin, statuary and all that, but he doesn't really know deep religion, not as Anna feels it. His is a religion of art and æstheticization, and a vague unknownness. *Black* is the key word as their marriage falls apart. He feels black, his blood boils with black, he sinks into a world of blackness (the allusions to the humours of Middles Ages medicine are apt). He realizes she is everything to him. '*Why* was she the all, the everything, why must he live only through her...?' (228). He can't escape her – he is still like a child (231). He comes to admire her beautiful pregnant belly, but he is still estranged (231).

As Anaïs Nin says, D.H. Lawrence is one of the first male writers to write about women authentically. What, then, about William Shakespeare, Catullus, Ovid, Francesco Petrarch, or Homer? But Lawrence gets deep inside his women characters. He is not saying, however, 'this is how women feel', but rather 'this is how *I think* women feel' – and within the context of a very particular kind of artwork, which tells a particular story, and via a narrator. (And written and published in a particular social context).

The Rainbow is deeply psychological, but it is not a psychoanalytical thesis or report. It is a psychological novel. It's fiction, not fact. D.H. Lawrence is just making stuff up. That's what authors do. But it has the philosophical authenticity of art. Art tries to get at the essence. In *The Rainbow*, Lawrence tries to get at the essence of modern women, and femininity, and marriage. His book can only be a one person's point-of-view, nothing more. It is Lawrence talking. He may be transcribing real women's feelings – Frieda Weekley's or his mother's or other women's, people he's known – but the result is still his – the product of a white, Western, bourgeois, 20th century writer born and raised in the English Midlands. He's just one person, among billions. Despite the multiple viewpoints in the fiction – Anna, Will, Tom, Ursula, Lydia – it's all one viewpoint, Lawrence's viewpoint.

D.H. Lawrence is equivocal, ambiguous. He tries as hard as he can to show the woman's feelings and point-of-view, but he is ambivalent about women. A feminist, a champion of women becoming 'self-responsible', he is also chauvinist and manipulative. Attacking patriarchy, he is also a victim of it (as everybody is who works and breathes within patriarchy – that is, same as everyone in the West). He attacks the system from within, but no one can stand completely outside of their culture. Enculturation is inescapable. But he tries, as an artist, to balance things. So Anna, who is a Goddess in full flight, who runs a mini-matriarchy in her house in *The Rainbow* (250), is balanced by Will and his dark cult of religious æsthetics, the Ruskinian man lingering on beyond his time.

D.H. Lawrence deals with opposites, with comparisons. He enjoys dialectical battles, dualisms, confrontations. It's the foundation of his entire philosophy. Thus his fiction is full of contrasts: Anna and Will, Ursula and Gudrun, Aaron and Lilly, and Mellors and Clifford. Places are opposed: typically Italy and England, or England and Mexico. Then the ideological confrontations: love and work, mind and body, nature and society, individual and crowd. And the philosophical oppositions: light and dark, inner and outer, masculine and feminine, etc. Lawrence is forever smashing two things together – the past and the present, love and labour, men and women.

Whatever happens, the old ways, the old world, must die. 'There must be a new world', asserts D.H. Lawrence (Moore, 422). I agree with him: the old ways must die (it's also the familiar cry of Surrealist art). Do away with them. Get fresh. Get some new ways, a new world. And this is the message in Lawrence's 1916 novel – whether you call it the return of mythic time, the re-instatement of the sacred, of Paradise, a new Christianity, a renascence of love and contact, the replacement of self with soul, it's really an urge towards a new life, a new world.

D.H. Lawrence calls this urge the new relation between man and woman, self-responsibility, a return to the source of life, transcendence of the ego, reaching beyond the self, a return to wholeness (Moore, 200, 273, 280-2, 302, 352), but it's all about the creation of a new world, a new life. (Sometimes Lawrence also called it getting into a proper relation with something).

D.H. Lawrence: Infinite Sensual Violence

How confident D.H. Lawrence was at this time, as he wrote *The Rainbow*. How visionary, how sure of his powers. As he works at it, during 1913 and after, he calls it 'strange' – clearly the new book surprised him. He began to be amazed by his own creation. We can follow his growing confidence in the letters. By April 22, 1914 he writes from Italy: 'It is a big and beautiful work' (Moore, 272). This is what makes *The Rainbow* a great book – because Lawrence was in ascension, moving up to the height of his powers. He doesn't go deeper or higher than *The Rainbow*. In many respects it's his finest work. Lawrence was working up to his apotheosis, as he writes in a letter of July 27, 1917 (III, 142):

> I knew, as I revised the book, that it was a kind of working up to the dark sensual or Dionysic or Aphrodic ecstasy, which does actually burst the world, burst the world-consciousness in every individual.

Big claims these, for just a novel. Few writers are so bombastic. D.H. Lawrence's idea – of bursting the world – would seem ridiculous if the book was bad. But the book is brilliant, and it's true.. (However, as film director Hayao Miyazaki noted, when you're creating, you have to think what you're doing is going to change the world).

D.H. Lawrence relied a lot on Edward Garnett when he was writing *The Rainbow*. Apart from his wife Frieda, Garnett seems to be the biggest influence on Lawrence at this time (1913-14). Lawrence was very concerned about Garnett's reaction to the book – this is clear from the letters. He hoped Garnett would like the work, and was defensive about it, taking pains to explain his creative decisions. He says he will rewrite the book in the third person (Moore, 208). Garnett's letters were very important to him, as he wrote the novel away from the source, in Germany and Italy.

But it's difficult to say too much about D.H. Lawrence's creative processes from the letters. Even though he was a prolific letter-writer, he didn't – he couldn't – put in everything he was working on. In any creative activity there is lot of thinking and behind-the-scenes work that doesn't end up in the artwork itself. Lawrence has an immensely quick mind. He made connections intuitively. He worked with his instinct. Hence the loose structure of his *œuvre* (poems, novels, essays). But even his swift pen couldn't capture all that went on in his head. Lawrence 'raided the inarticulate' like any artist, but he was more articulate than most. This always strikes me: he is so articulate, so fluid, so descriptive, so vivid.

Matriarchy battles with patriarchy. D.H. Lawrence is ambivalent about both social, psychosexual systems. In *The Rainbow*, matriarchy grows out of patriarchy, symbolized by Lydia out of Tom, Anna out of Will (or is it vice versa?). It is significant that Anna identifies herself with Tom, and Ursula with Will (the father-daughter relation is vital in both sets of relationships, and both Ursula and Anna have something of a father fixation, which partly plays into their neurosis. That is, some of their psychological problems stem from their ambiguous relations with their fathers. Well, all of Lawrence's female charas are father complex women). And, after the death of Tom, Ursula goes to her grandmother, now an old crone-figure, a wise Goddess (297). The old matriarch says she hopes someone will love Ursula for what she *is*, not for what he desires of her (304). The distinction is significant, for the novel describes people coming into being, not through action but through self-realization. Lawrence is after beingness; he cares for 'what the woman *is* – what she is – inhumanly, psychologically, materially' (Moore, 282). The battle in *The Rainbow* is between matriarchy and patriarchy, played out on the personal level by men and women. As Julian Moynahan comments in *The Deed of Life: The Novels and Tales of D.H. Lawrence*: 'the crucial relation in *The Rainbow* is between a man and a woman in marital and sexual experience' (43).

The birth of being is strived for in *The Rainbow*. Anna does not quite attain it. She stops short on the journey (237). But she does attain a detached self (242), as Will does. Anna becomes the Earth-Goddess: 'She felt like the earth, the mother of everything' (250). When Anna and

D.H. Lawrence: Infinite Sensual Violence

Will make love passion sinks towards death. It is all fierce blackness, 'a sensuality violent and extreme as death'. It is summed up in that extraordinary phrase of Lawrence's: 'infinite sensual violence' (280). Nothing half-hearted in Lawrence's art here: *infinite sensual violence*, three powerful words strung together. It is a vicious, deathly phrase, having more to do with fascism or power than with love.

※

Traditionally, the break in the 1916 novel is seen by critics occurring at the end of "The Marsh and the Flood" chapter. In fact, "The Cathedral" chapter is really the end of the first half of *The Rainbow*. From "The Child" chapter onwards the centre of gravity of the book shifts. The writing changes. The rest of the novel, from pages 253–548, belongs to Ursula Brangwen.

The spirit of patriarchy breathes through Ursula. She reacts to maleness, and part of her yearning for being is fuelled by knowing the male – her father – early on:

> The return or the departure of the father was the one event which the child remembered. When he came, something woke in her, some yearning. (261)

For much of the 1916 novel Ursula tries to get in contact with the male. The very early state of infancy with her father scars her for life. She never quite gets back to it. Childhood is always the Golden Age of civilizations. In *The Rainbow* D.H. Lawrence tries to placate the œdipal tensions, to work through the complexity of the parent-child relation, and how this relation must open out, in ever-widening circles, to embrace marriage, the grown child, other relations, and further out to the self-and-society relation. The book is a set of interconnecting relationships, and the model for these relations is a series of inter-locking circles and spirals. The rainbow is meant to bridge the gaps between them, whether the rainbow is an arch, a door, a Cathedral or a curve of seven blazing spiritual colours.

Tom dies, and Ursula is born. There is a transmigration of souls (of hearts, of minds, of power, of interest) from Tom to Ursula, the first and the last people in the 1916 book, the beginning and the end, the alpha and the omega. Tom, the ancient patriarch, is all Western life from the time of the ancient civilizations of Egypt, Sumer and Greece to the mediæval era. Will is the Renaissance man, the humanist, the lover of beauty (but he is too æstheticized, too reliant upon an artistic or philosophical way of looking at the world). Will brings the parable up to modern times, and Ursula is the embodiment of the modern world, the modern sensibility. All the tensions and anxieties of the modern West rage in her, the proto-feminism, the post-New Woman feminism, the emerging independence for women.

With Tom's heroic death, the old world dies finally, and the new world, embodied in Ursula, is ushered in. A reluctant culture bearer, Ursula has to assimilate the pains of living in the modern world in a new way. Some of her anxieties are eternal ones, ones Tom and everyone before him had to deal with, but she is also faced with new ones.

Tom dies, and, through Lydia, Ursula absorbs his life. The weight of the past is heavy upon her, as in Australian aboriginal dreamtime, but it is not as spacious or as challenging as the future. Unlike Will, Ursula is not a Ruskinite, exalting the Gothic Past. Will is like Jude Fawley, and Ursula is like Sue Bridehead. Of all books, *The Rainbow* is most like *Jude the Obscure* (it's virtually a sequel, or a reworking of the same material).

In *Jude the Obscure,* Thomas Hardy parodies the *New Testament.* Sue Bridehead is an unwilling Virgin Mary, and Jude Fawley is a martyred Joseph, the ineffective father figure. In *The Rainbow,* D.H. Lawrence again takes up the multi-layered problem of the nuclear family in which each member is struggling to become religious, to make the Holy Family. Anna, Ursula, Theresa, Catherine – the names Lawrence chooses for the children are all supremely Christian names, the names of women saints, Ursula and Catherine being famous martyred saints in the Catholic canon. So Lydia is St Anne, the mother of Mary, the powerful matriarch, the wise crone, the Black Goddess. Lydia, like St

D.H. Lawrence: Infinite Sensual Violence

Anne, is full of otherness, of a power that comes from some Mysterious Elsewhere. Tom is Noah and Joachim, the patriarch with the macho exterior but who is interiorly a slave to Woman. Anna is Mary, the Goddess as Eternal Mother. And Ursula is Jesus – which's utterly right in Lawrence's deeply feminized worldview.

There is something of Mary Magdalene too about Ursula. The aim of Mary Magdalene is (partly) to create a deep relation with her beloved, Jesus, just as Ursula tries to do with Winifred and Anton. In his letters Bertie Lawrence says that Jesus (and us) would be better off if he stuck with Mary Magdalene instead of the disciples. Jesus loving Mary Magdalene – it's still something that upsets many people (remember the great controversy surrounding the 1988 movie *The Last Temptation of Christ*, or the blockbuster novel *The Da Vinci Code*). It's a problem – the sexualization of Christ – that the Gnostics tackled (in the Cathars, Rosicrucians and Magdalene cults of the Middle Ages). D.H. Lawrence took up the problem head-on in *The Escaped Cock*, giving Jesus a mate. It's the eternal issue of the human couple, the Gnostic *syzygy*, the two yokes (souls) in the same egg (love), the King and Queen and Black and White of alchemy and Taoism. Fusing the two, the masculine and feminine, is ever the West's concern. In magical cults, from the Egyptian and Greek religions down through the ages to the present day, the problem of love is seen in religious terms. It is no less religious in Lawrence's novels, though the settings – the industrial English Midlands – are thoroughly secular.

※

So innocent Ursula is. She gets all the best lines, phrases of speech that are instantly memorable:

- "I could never die while there was a tree"
- "If I were the moon, I know where I would fall down"
- "Do you feel like a bird blown out of its own latitude?"

(338, 379, 382)

The answer to everything Ursula says is *Yes*. Yes, Ursula, yes! Go to work, go to teach, go to college, love Winifred, love Anthony, love Anton, yes yes yes!

She talks like a child – sweet and memorable and infuriating. Yes yes yes – say yes to everything.

D.H. Lawrence says that the love-union must occur on a religious plane, and must require a death and a rebirth. His characters – from Paul Morel in 1913's *Sons and Lovers* to Connie Chatterley in 1928's *Lady Chatterley's Lover* – die and are reborn.

The death must be part suicide and part murder. It must come from within (suicide), but also because society wills it (murder). Thus Tom's epic death in *The Rainbow* is part-suicide, part-murder. The natural world, as the Flood, overtakes him, but his life is rounded-out. His deep self is ready to die, although his body and his blood-intimacy struggles against death. It's absolutely right that his demise should be plum in the middle of his homeland. He drifts right past Lydia. He goes back into the earth, just like a dying seed, to be reborn, just as Jesus says. The seed falls, dies, and brings forth fruit (*The Gospel of John*, 12:24).

The Flood is the water from the Goddess's womb, the life-blood. Tom notes this before he dies; he thinks of the eternal permanence of water (288). Water, whether ocean, river, flood or rain, is nature-in-motion, the life-energy. Tom goes back into the Earth, into the Goddess, into the waters of the world-womb. Lydia, his life-blood and rebirther, presides over this mythic transformation. It's a traumatic scene, necessarily for the sense of drama, but symbolically it is momentous. The women in Tom's life apotheosize him afterwards, but the men feel rage (294).

Tom's death in the Flood causes mythical ripples to spread all round his falling body – those widening circles. As the great force of patriarchy in *The Rainbow*, in the figure of Tom, falls out of the narrative, the trinity of matriarchal figures is highlighted: Lydia – Anna – Ursula, a trio of grandmother–mother–daughter. Will seems to be left on his own, surrounded by Anna, Ursula and his many daughters (and one son). Will is no patriarch – Anna cuts him down, says her father is worth more than ten of his kind. The female figures get stronger and stronger in *The Rainbow* – from Lydia through to Ursula, while the men from Tom through Will to Anton, get weaker. They lack self-assertion, Will and Anton, and in battles with the feminine principle, they afterwards retreat into hardness. They lack guts, they lack the will to beingness, which is what the women possess. D.H. Lawrence later tries to even this up in his subsequent fiction, with his male leaders – Gerald, Kangaroo, and Cipriano (in the so-called 'leadership' novels). By the time of *Lady Chatterley's Lover,* Lawrence seems no closer to resolving the man<–>woman conflict. Mellors still retains much of the proto-fascism of Lawrence's leaders, while Connie reverts to a pre-*Rainbow* femininity, a willingness to be led by the male, to give up her self-responsibility. Discussing the 'leadership' novels in "Making the Classics Contemporary", L.D. Clark suggests a new grouping, of 'pilgrimage' novels:

> ...a more rewarding procedure would be to group together all six novels between *Women In Love* and *Lady Chatterley's Lover*: *Aaron's Rod* – which I put first because Lawrence began it first – *The Lost Girl, Mr Noon, Kangaroo, The Boy in the Bush* and *The Plumed Serpent.* I will refer to these as 'pilgrimage' novels. All of them aim at rebirth of the human soul, through new access to the power of instinct, access gained only by pilgrimage from a wasteland to a land of regeneration: 'thought adventure' must be realised in geographic adventure. (in P. Preston, 192)

Another rebirth-by-water occurs in *The Horse-Dealer's Daughter.* Here the mother and daughter are glorified. Mabel is alone in the patriarchal world of her self-satisfied, surly brothers, but 'she seemed in a sort of ecstasy to be coming nearer to her fulfilment, her own glorification, approaching her dead mother, who was glorified' (CSS, 419).

The imagery in The *Horse-Dealer's Daughter* is powerful, very Thomas Hardyan – the dead land, the dead pool, the black figure – but the resurrection love-scene is pure D.H. Lawrence. There is a real strangeness in Lawrence's use of water – in the drowning sequence in *Women In Love,* for instance, so powerfully filmed by Ken Russell & co. (the lovers entwined in the mud of the drained lake). Or the scene in

Sons and Lovers where Paul and Clara make love. Or the rapturous scene in *Lady Chatterley's Lover* where Connie and Mellors run through the rain. And the greatest scene, when Ursula stands in the surf and yells, "'I want to go!'" (R, 531)

Ursula's desire is for selfhood, total beingness. Eugene Goodheart commented in 1991:

> The desire for autonomy, for a self-posessed solitude can be understood as a defense against the importunities of desire. To be autonomous is to constitute one's own world, create one's desires, and control their satisfaction. In order to achieve this autonomy, the self must assert its superiority and indifference to the world. (66)

Ursula has to decide between the confines of love and the (de)limitations of 'freedom', to choose between love and solitude, between two different prisons, each hedged about with their own problems. In *Women In Love,* Birkin describes the will to being as a dying-to-self, the self-denial that mystics speak of:

> "There's the whole difference in the world," he said, "between the actual sensual being, and the vicious mental-deliberate profligacy our lot goes in for. in our night time, there's always the electricity switched on, we watch ourselves, we get it all in the head, really. You've got to lapse out before you can know what sensual reality is, lapse into unknowingness, and give up your volition. You've got to do it. you've got to learn not-to-be, before you can come into being." (94)

Ursula is all *yearning*. The word sums her up. She is all for the ultimate (320). She asks poignant questions: 'Where was the ecstasy?' (324). She quivers with 'passionate yearning' (331). She craves for Christ. Well, if she can't have him, then how about a Lancelot-figure, the mythical knight in shining armour? No, instead she gets Anton Skrebensky. He makes her quiver. He certainly upsets the equilibrium of her world. With his arrival a racial circle of life is completed – the Polish connection, that sense of the Beyond, the Outside, which she inherits through Anna from her grandmother.

Ursula is all yearning – a bird blown out of her latitude, while

D.H. Lawrence: Infinite Sensual Violence

Anton is supremely complacent (338). In some ways this is all D.H. Lawrence can do with her – fill her with yearning. His writing changes with Ursula's story: it becomes looser, it loses some of its momentum. The sequence at the end of the chapter "The Widening Circle" is a good example. This is pure Lawrencean polemic, written in a familiar first-person intuitive style. Who is the voice? Not Ursula. Lawrence here intrudes: 'Can I not, then, walk this earth in gladness...?' (326). Not Ursula, this voice. Her thought, yes, but this is no interior monologue. Lawrence ruins the diegetic effect here. This first part of the book, though intensely psychological, has been more in the manner of the traditional novel. With Ursula the realm is all psychic, the novel becomes modern.

With Ursula's story, D.H. Lawrence gets to the heart of his 1916 book, the heart of his art, his life's work. Ursula's story is a series of disillusionments. First religion, Christ and the church fail her. Then her mother, who lives in fecundity (Peter Paul Rubens is absolutely right for the image of blood-intimacy gone wild – those cascades of overripe nude bodies in Rubens' paintings). Then her father fails her. With her job Ursula finally breaks away from the parents. She tries to placate them with money, but the results are uneasy. She is out in the world. This world too is painful and disappointing.

Anton Skrebensky is the first major disillusionment. Ursula is a sleeping beauty (345), a fairy tale princess waiting to be sexually awakened. Alas, he is no Lancelot, no phallic Grail Knight. He is no Tristan. As Jack Zipes notes in *The Brothers Grimm*, in fairy tales such as *Cinderella*, *Sleeping Beauty* and *Snow White*, the male hardly features: he appears at the end to provide the proper closure by 'rationally, morally or cunningly ordering her world [so that it] becomes his world' (73). The man is the icing on the cake, to round off the story. Zipes writes that, for the heroine of fairy tales

> the male is her reward, and it is apparent that, even though he is an incidental character, he arrives on the scene to take over, to govern and control her future (ib., 64)

As with Anna and Will, Ursula is disappointed by Anton's seeming social indifference. The past is with her, all around her. D.H. Lawrence notes this in a fashion Thomas Hardy would approve of:

> ...they continued to walk on, quivering like shadows under the ash-trees of the hill, where her grandfather had walked with his daffodils to make his proposal, and where her mother had gone with her young husband, walking close upon him as Ursula was now walking upon Skrebensky. (345)

Into their young romance D.H. Lawrence throws all his powers, all the pyrotechnics of prose he knows:

> She was very beautiful then, so wide opened, so radiant, so palpitating, exquisitely vulnerable and poignantly, wrongly, throwing herself at risk (348)

This is the D.H. Lawrence of *Lady Chatterley's Lover,* the vibrant prose stylist who veers from rapture to ranting. But Lawrence is great in the description of this love affair. No one else writes '[i]n her bedroom she threw her arms in the air, in clear pain of magnificence' (353). But when it comes to the moonlit annihilation sequence, Lawrence seems to fudge it. All those exclamation marks, the 'oh-oh-ohs', the flood of superlatives – it's all too much. Too much of it in the prose, as in the emotions. Clearly he's grabbing at something beyond speech. Yes, we know that. But he doesn't continue in that stately style of Anna and Will's rhythmic, cornfield scene. Instead, Lawrence goes wild.

As with Anna, the moon bursts in upon Ursula. Of course it does: she is a Moon-Goddess, and the Goddess rides her, in the Gravesian sense of Muses (the Goddess 'rides' a woman who's a Muse for Graves). She wants to go, to be gone, into the Beyond. She will yell this later in the surf (531). Now the darkness surges around her. The setting is again Hardyan – a wedding, with music and dancing, the moon, the stacks of corn. It is a carnival time, the Saturnalia, Chaos Night, when chaos overturns order, and D.H. Lawrence doesn't hang around to whip up the ecstasy. He starts in with it, at full pitch, and keeps it there. Ursula feels madness inside her. But Skrebensky steps between her and the moon, her source of power, the Beyond. At this point, as she rises to her full power, she needs something majestic and deep. Sadly, Anton cannot provide it. Perhaps nobody and nothing can. The important thing for Ursula is that the yearning is there. She can't control it. It sweeps through her like a flood, like the flood in *The Virgin and the Gipsy,* like the horses will do later on in *The Rainbow.* She is, as we all are, a child of nature, and when nature overtakes her, whether it is hormones or menstruation or simply a big appetite for life, she can't help herself.

At this point, she needs a shaman or witch to help her, someone to take her as far she can go. Ursula is indeed a shaman in the making, a shamaness having her first major psycho-religious trauma. The language is of shamanic, religious ecstasy: light, fire, the moon, communion, heat, typically Lawrencean but also typical of world religions throughout the ages since their origins in shamanism. Ursula should be guided to go beyond, to embrace what she yearns for. Instead, Anton pulls her away from the moon (365). He denies all this magical seething inside her. It would be better if Merlin appeared, or a priestess of Isis or Hecate or Diana. What is she doing with a soldier, the epitome of the secular world, the right-wing, military machine? She needs magic, a love-magician.

No wonder Ursula annihilates Anton. Her deep energy is misdirected. He asks for sex, for attention ("Don't you like me tonight?" "Leave me alone", she answers [366]). In the dance she goes into a trance. He doesn't leave her alone, as he should. He doesn't know what she's feeling. Ursula can't tell him. Many of her problems, many of our problems, stem from an inability to articulate these deep feelings.

She freezes. Her energy is misguided, and turns into cold metal. She should be allowed to go with the basic mythic, shamanic experience, to run with it, but he intrudes with his demands for sex. She is much more developed than he is at this point. He is not ready for such depth. He tries to assert the male blood-relation, through secular desire. But she has gone far beyond that. His frustration is that he doesn't know what she wants – he can't apprehend it. Her frustration, which turns to rage, is that she can't (and doesn't really want to) tell him.

She's gone, he can't go. The Beyond (the moon) is only to be experienced by the individual. He tries to control it all, to 'net her brilliant, cold, self-burning body' while she wants to 'make him into nothing' (367-8).

So D.H. Lawrence crystallizes one of the basic human tensions in the man<–>woman relationship, at the heart of love in the Western world from Ovid onwards: *the man wants something the woman will not give; the woman wants something the man cannot give.*

It's a really, really powerful piece of writing, D.H. Lawrence at his best. But it's still disappointing. You want him to go further, to push the scene even further, even deeper. He came back to this material in *Women In Love*, and in *Lady Chatterley's Lover*, but he still hadn't quite cracked it. We can see how much it obsessed him, making him compose three versions of *Lady Chatterley's Lover*. But he never got there. He was still tackling it right to the end, in *The Escaped Cock*, in *Lady Chatterley's Lover* and *Apocalypse*.

The moon-annihilation scene powers the 1916 novel up to a new, more intense religious level. Directly after the scene Ursula is battling with the state, religion, the *Bible*, and God. Again, as with any student, her questions indicate the level of her thinking, they tell us where she is.

"'After all, how big was the Flood?'" she asks (372). Well, Ursula, the Flood was small compared to you. All the big changes and the big challenges occur on the inside, in the heart and mind and soul, in the Lawrencean world.

All this questioning – of war, work, religion, God, love, etc – makes sense only through the character of Ursula. She is at the centre of the book as is Tess Durbeyfield in *Tess of the d'Urbervilles*. Both heroines

D.H. Lawrence: Infinite Sensual Violence

question life. D.H. Lawrence is always strident, polemical, even in his lyricism. He knows and uses softness, but only to set up the big, polemical fires he'll ignite on the next page. *The Rainbow* – and most of Lawrence's fiction – works best when he keeps his fiery polemic under control, and burns it inside his characters. Smouldering rather than rampaging fires. Some of Ursula's theological arguments are marred by authorial intrusions (just as Anton intrudes upon Ursula with sex). So when Ursula says she loves lions not lambs, it works well (389). The lamb is all gentleness and innocence. If they're not slaughtered, symbolically or for real, they grow up to be tame sheep.

Lions, meanwhile, signify royalty, splendour, fire, heat, and courage, as well as evil and cruelty. Lions eat Christians, and battle unicorns and dragons. The lion is the Goddess's animal, too, associated with Artemis, Cybele, Tara and the Gorgon. The lion is clearly the male, the *animus*, in Ursula, her soul-fire, the God-image, her dæmon, the Christ and Lancelot inside her.

> She stretched her own limbs like a lion or a wild horse, her heart relentless in its desires. (390)

The teacher Winifred Inger is a kind of helper. She helps Ursula to grow. She is not a shamaness or a witch, but she has a coven of women around her – the Woman's Movement. Constant conflict in the 1910s novel continues. Ursula sees the ugliness of the houses on the way to Wiggiston (392). The visionary, Apocalyptic Lawrence is foregrounded more and more. England is no New Jerusalem, the place is instead full of dark, Satanic mills, factories and disgusting industries. All of this is welcome in Lawrence's art because it's all true. The Midlands of England is a hideous place. Formless, squalid, meaningless, unliving, ghoulish, inane – Lawrence loves to despise contemporary England. He's right. It's true. It is horrible (and it's far worse now than it was in the 1910s and 1920s).

Then comes the fight in *The Rainbow* with the parents over work. The dreams, the reality, and the distance between them. She fantasizes about Gillingham in Kent (409), but this is as gruesome as any of D.H. Lawrence's worst nightmares (it's still a dreadfully squalid town). "The Man's World" chapter, about Ursula's first job of being a teacher, is a terrific Descent Into Hell. How well Lawrence speaks of teaching – the conflicts, the ugliness, the meanness, the stupidity. Again, Lawrence can't be too harsh here because it's all true, it's happening right now (and of course Lawrence had his own experiences as a teacher to draw upon). So Ursula moves beyond religion, the parents, the family and home, beyond love into the degradation of daily work.

Work is 'ghastly', D.H. Lawrence wrote in *Study of Thomas Hardy* (32). When the work is done, what then? he asks. You must get on with the real business of life – living (38). I agree. Work in the left-wing/Communist view is prostitution in the Western capitalist system. It's for the machine, it's not real, but it's back-breaking. Lorenzo was not against decent work, getting in touch with your body, with the 'flow of warmth, affection and physical unison', as he remarked in "Men Must Work and Women As Well" (SP, 421).

How battered Ursula gets working in the school in *The Rainbow*. It's all distressing and dispiriting. It kills the soul. You become a zombie, one of the 'mute and grey' commuters (471). You still see them today, at London Bridge, Shinjuku, Grand Central stations – rows and rows of commuters, trains full of them. Ursula is moving away from the stereotypes of women within patriarchy. She is becoming, as Sue Bridehead is in Thomas Hardy's *Jude the Obscure*, a 'New Woman'. Carolyn Heilbrun writes (in *Towards a Recognition of Androgyny*) that Ursula is a New Woman who is 'entirely alone' at the end of the novel (109-110).

Mr Harby the headmaster is an authentic creation in *The Rainbow* – not because he's so cruel but because he doesn't want to be there, like so many teachers. It's a battle of wills. The classroom still is a battle-ground today. D.H. Lawrence's portrayal of the sly, smirking kids as well as the tired, harassed teachers, is spot-on. People are forced into

D.H. Lawrence: Infinite Sensual Violence

holes, it's a prison. Inmates and warders. Slavery. Society in miniature it must be, because of all the jobs Ursula could have done, Lawrence chose teaching. Education is society here. A hospital or a factory or a mining pit would have worked just as well. The irony about a school being a location of the chapter "The Man's World" in *The Rainbow* is that education is one of the few professions where women predominate (but not in the top jobs).

So, the hard way, Ursula learns to keep her real, personal self out of it, to put on the po-faced mask everyone else attaches in the morning before catching the bus to work (445). The price is high, to her soul (455), and D.H. Lawrence shows so well how difficult it is to return to the self you were before work, to recapture your early ecstasies.

> She was in revolt. For once, she was free, she could get somewhere. Ah, the wonderful, real somewhere that was beyond her, the somewhere she felt deep, deep inside her. (456)

She does get back to ecstasy, to her self, to flowers and deep life (470), but at great cost.

Ursula's circle of life in *The Rainbow* continues to open out. She has already met a whole new set of people in the provinces (390). D.H. Lawrence himself was one of these. Dissatisfaction is the hallmark of the people in Lawrence's novels, as it is in those of André Gide, Albert Camus, Samuel Beckett and Lawrence Durrell. 'Paul was dissatisfied with himself and with everything', as it's summarized in *Sons and Lovers* (SL, 27). It is the modern human condition in fiction (taken to extremes in mid-20th century Existentialist novels), but is by no means new. People have *always* lived in states of anxiety. Lawrence simply brings this restlessness into focus. It is new in literature, perhaps, being associated with modernism. (However, the characters in the first novel in the West, *Satyricon* by Petronius, are fairly unhappy and anxious).

The episode with Anthony in *The Rainbow* is rather pathetic. He is an even further watered-down male, a pale shadow of Anton Skrebensky (who is a shadow of Will, who is a shadow of Tom, etc). They're all shadows, right back to Christ, or Adam, the first man. As Ursula completes the seasonal cycle at the school, she is a 'bird that had learned in some measure to fly' (467). She is not yet ready to fly off utterly. Flying is one of *the* symbols of freedom. D.H. Lawrence uses it again a few pages later: Ursula wants 'to be free to fly her kite as high as she liked' (469). Of course: there's no ceiling to the sky. There the law cannot reach. How we'd like to let her fly, to help her take off. But where? she doesn't know, we don't know. We are no nearer to knowing at the end of the book. The yearning is the thing. The yearning comes first, and maybe last.

'The aspiration was the real thing', Ursula Brangwen thinks in *The Rainbow* (389), and again: 'Out of the far, far space there had drifted slowly in to her a passionate, unborn yearning' (483). Like Jude Fawley in Thomas Hardy's final novel, Ursula builds up an image of college life. It can never be fulfilled. College becomes a factory for increasing one's career prospects, a stepping-stone merely (486). Ursula is still asking basic, yearning questions, such as: *Is That All?* ('Was life like this, and this only?' [ib.]). Who hasn't asked or thought this question? Is this all, is this *really* everything there is? Yes. The moon landings are sixty years off, but things won't change that much.

This *is* everything. Right here, right now.

Only part of Ursula believes that. Like most souls on the planet, she's sure there's got to be Something More Than This.

At this point, as D.H. Lawrence wonders where his 1916 novel is going to go, and how to end it, he gives us a summary of Ursula's life and her position. The next move might be out into the world again, but she is still Ursula Brangwen. Is she, and the novel, never going to end? No: it and she carry on, and on, and on.

Ursula's anger drives her onward. 'Lawrence consistently depicts the natural female state as furious rebellion', remarked Carol Siegel in *Lawrence Among the Women* (16). Ursula never stops. The novel never stops. Lawrence never stops (he worked over the same problems up to

D.H. Lawrence: Infinite Sensual Violence

his death). The criticism never stops. Life never stops.

❋

So she's opened-up again. In steps Anton Skrebensky the soldier. Why him? Why not someone bigger? For, although he's changed, he hasn't acquired any more depth. Only a materialistic, dumb reply to Ursula's heartfelt letter with the words, "I am married".

He comes from the secular world of light and reason while she flies in the outer, sacred darkness. At any moment the darkness could rush in, if only people would let it. But all the barriers are up. No one lets the darkness in, nor throws firebrands out into it (488). Damn it, everyone's too limited. The circle ain't widening for them.

So Ursula B. takes Anton S. into the darkness. It's big, and the kisses flow (497). For a while she feels great, a leopard crying madly in the night (499). But the hot flow of fecundity is something she despised once – in her mother, and the Brangwens. After what she's been through, it's bound to be bliss. It doesn't last, but later she sees her mother in a 'just and true light'. Her mother had simply accepted the life given her. Ursula realizes the greatness in this, but she herself cannot keep still. 'I must have the moon in my keeping', she thinks (537).

The kisses and the blisses continue for a while in *The Rainbow* – the lovers live in a honeymoon world, a short spell in Paradise. Their love-making is full of darkness and whirling wind (501). They make love now outside, beyond the family and the home, and at night (501-2). Lawlessness reigns for a while, and nothing can hold them back. The forces of pure nature run through them (as the horses will do later through Ursula).

The writing here has a magnificence about it as D.H. Lawrence turns on the power to finish his novel:

> She passed away as on a dark wind, far, far away, into the pristine darkness of paradise, into the original immortality. She entered the dark fields of immortality. (502)

London, Sussex, Rouen, they begin to take in the world, to make it theirs. At Rouen, the church image returns, and the darkness pushes Ursula beyond Anton.

The crisis comes in *The Rainbow*, and it pivots around marriage. The dream is shattered. Anton wants to possess Ursula, in the unholy, dishonourable, slave-making, materialist, patriarchal state of matrimony, and let no one rend them asunder, *amen*. They've been tupping like mad in hotels everywhere, but they haven't really connected. He hasn't really known what she was thinking. Of course, our Urtler says NEVER to marriage. And here Lawrence only repeats what has been said a billion times before – that sexual union does not always mean soul union. There is always antagonism, as there is in Lawrence's symbols, when he uses symbols of detachment and distance: 'the star-equilibrium excludes the happy movements of intimacy,' writes Chong-Wha Chung in "In Search of the Dark God: Lawrence's Dualism", 'as the stars are forever fixed in polarisation. It is the same lion and the unicorn are fighting eternally without any chance of uniting together' (in P. Preston, 72).

The Ursula-Skrebensky relationship is corrosive and confused to the end. Peter Balbert remarks in *D.H. Lawrence: A Centenary Consideration*:

> The history of Ursula's long affair with Skrebensky, which concludes with the antipothalamic trappings of a miscarriage, an emasculated male, and a sick female, stands as Lawrence's warning of the pathology in a love that does not produce a joint singling out. (1985, 59)

Anton weeps all the way from Richmond to Hyde Park. The prewedding love-making is Thomas Hardy's fiction eroticized. The most significant element here is the ocean. It breathes into Ursula. It fills her with passion. The ocean connects her with every other place on the planet. You can step onto it and go anywhere; it is an ever-shifting Yellow Brick Road.

The passion of the sea burns into her. She yearns for the Beyond

D.H. Lawrence: Infinite Sensual Violence

again. What a terrific image it is, the best in the 1916 novel, of Ursula Brangwen prowling along in the surf. All the motifs in the novel are featured here: the moon, fire, metal, whiteness, darkness, water, and the circle (of the ocean):

> "How wonderful!" cried Ursula, in low, calling tones. "How wonderful!"
> And she went forward, plunging into it. He followed behind. She too seemed to melt into the glare, towards the moon.
> The sands were as ground silver, the sea moved in solid brightness, coming towards them, and she went to meet the advance of the flashing, buoyant water. She gave her breast to the moon, her belly to the flashing, heaving water. He stood behind, encompassed, a shadow ever dissolving.
> She stood on the edge of the water, at the edge of the solid, flashing body of the sea, and the wave rushed over her feet.
> "I want to go," she cried, in a strong, dominant voice. "I want to go."
> He saw the moonlight on her face, so she was like metal, he heard her ringing, metallic voice, like the voice of a harpy to him.
> She prowled, ranging on the edge of the water like a possessed creature, and he followed her. He saw the froth of the wave followed by the hard, bright water swirl over her feet and her ankles, she swung out her arms, to balance, he expected every moment to see her walk into the sea, dressed as she was, and be carried swimming out.
> But she turned, she walked to him.
> "I want to go," she cried, in the high, hard voice, like the scream of gulls.
> "Where?" he asked.
> "I don't know." (531)

The Great Yearning bursts in her, burns in her.

And she annihilates him, again. And that's the end of it. No more. No more of that nonsense.

After the bitterness of ecstasy, she repents, she feels wrong (536). And, repentant, like a martyred saint, she writes a burning letter to him, just as Tess Durbeyfield wrote to Angel Clare before she killed Alec d'Urberville in *Tess of the d'Urbervilles* (the murder of Alec was another annihilation beside the ocean – in Sandbourne).

The water comes again in *The Rainbow* – the ocean floods the land and in the cold wetness she meets the horses – a living, animal Flood. How big will the Flood be? Ursula had asked earlier. Well, when it does come, it is with phallic, shadowy power. It has to occur under oak trees, the phallic, royal trees of England.

The description of the horses is fierce – fierce, fiery writing. The imagery is all sex: *darkness, wetness, massive, redness, clenched* and *bursting* are the words used (540). It's like the infamous phallic 'hunting-out' sequence in *Lady Chatterley's Lover* (a thorough-going purgation).

Ursula Brangwen climbs up the phallus, the oak tree. It's not Anton that impregnates her, but the horses. The child she thinks is inside her is really herself, her new self. She is giving birth to herself. She is a parthenogenic Goddess, needing not a male but nature to seed her. The natural realm, in all its wildness, courses through her. There's no image terrifyingly wilder than a group of horses running through a field. They are angels of darkness.

Socially and culturally, Ursula Brangwen has come through the meat grinder of Western culture; she has been through the whole, very painful enculturation process. Rejecting so many things, Ursula comes out on the other side relatively intact. 'Having rejected the institution of compulsory heterosexuality, aligned and then thrown the political prize of lesbian practice and sexuality between women out with the decaying world,' writes Nigel Kelsey in *D.H. Lawrence: Sexual Crisis*:

> the major quest of the text which seeks to discover who exactly is going to emancipate her seems wholly incongruous knowing as we do now, that the 'who' is firmly enclosed within a subject-subject relationship. In this instance a man, coming 'from the Infinite and she should hail him'. (140)

It is sad that D.H. Lawrence is still, at the very end of *The Rainbow*, conjuring up men as companions to women, as if the lessons of the agonies of compulsory heterosexuality haven't been learnt. Yet the radiant, visionary quality of the text at this point in *The Rainbow* overwhelms and transcends mere sexual stereotypes.

*

Ursula is rebirthed. She has nothing, she has everything: 'I have no father nor mother nor lover, I have no allocated place in the world of things', but she does have a seed inside, a great, swollen seed, and it bursts (545). It's excellent. She begins again from scratch, from nothing. She owns nothing, and nobody owns her. She is a free agent. She can run into the future, into the Beyond. She is accomplished. The world is hers because it is not hers. She claims nothing yet has everything. She can give birth to herself. She is a Goddess. There is nothing to be afraid of. There never *was* anything to be afraid of. She is a naked seed. She is growing. Birth is all about her.

> She slept breathing with her soul the new air of the new world. The peace was very deep and everything expands. (546)

She grows, she expands, everything expands. The Glory is inside her. She absorbs the world, the arch, the circle, the rainbow. She sees germination in all things (547), even in the hideous English Midlands. She has the rainbow inside her. The rainbow, which signifies spiritual riches and deep contact, has been accomplished. At this point, Christ says "It is finished". But Ursula is just beginning.

D.H. Lawrence and Frieda Weekley

D.H. Lawrence in Italy, at Villa Mirenda

4

Being Reborn

Strange, that the urgent will in me, to set
My mouth on hers in kisses, and so softly
To bring together two strange sparks, beget

Another life from our lives, so should send
The innermost fire of my own dim soul out-spinning
And whirling in blossom of flame and being upon me!

...The seed is purpose, blossom accident.
The seed is all in all, the blossom lent
To crown the triumph of this new descent.

D.H. Lawrence, 'Roses of All the World' (*Poems*, 218)

Being is D.H. Lawrence's goal, not doing. Like Andre Gide and Rainer Maria Rilke, Lawrence says 'be thyself', not 'know thyself' (P2, 456). *Be thyself* – this is the imperative that drives characters such as Ursula, Paul, Kate, Connie, Somers, Aaron and Birkin. Being, not doing. In this sense, Lawrence is a mystical writer – complete being is the goal of most mysticisms. The aim is to achieve beingness, a full sense of being, through self-realization and self-transcendence. Anyone can *do*, argues Lawrence, but few can *be*. 'Mystic equality lies in being, not in having or in doing, which are process', he wrote in *Women In Love* (299).

D.H. Lawrence: Infinite Sensual Violence

For D.H. Lawrence, being was not ideal or spiritual, but 'as much material as existence' (SP, 454-5). For Lawrence, being has substance. It is an experience, not an abstraction. Lawrence has always been concerned with being and how to achieve it. He says all of Thomas Hardy's characters are 'struggling to come into being' (TH, 20). Being for Lawrence is a mode of living that is intuitive, indescribable, whole and deep. Being is not mere existence. That is not enough. There must be more. Being is in essence being alive – more and more alive.

There is a wonderful argument in *Study of Thomas Hardy*, typical of D.H. Lawrence, where he asks *why work?* Work is necessary for food and clothing, sure. But what then? What happens after work?

> Living is not simply not-dying. It is the only real thing, it is the aim and end of all life. (TH, 38)

D.H. Lawrence's complaint was that in the modern world we aren't really alive anymore. We are half-dead. We're zombies. We've got to wake up (but whether humans were ever truly alive in the first place, in Lawrence's sense, is not so certain: often Lawrence projects into the past, and claims that, for instance, the Etruscans seemed to be really alive). It's a common complaint in modern literature, and is only to a degree a projection of an individual writer's own being, own mood, own unhappiness. It's true. You can't say that other people are dead-while-alive. You can say that it seems to you that everyone seems dead. But they're not. Everyone feels pain, hunger, fear, anxiety – and every other emotion. All too often Lawrence projected his fears onto the world. But we know what he means.

What is life? Let people decide for themselves, D.H. Lawrence said, and went on to define life for himself: life is contact, consciousness (P1, 289), it is a 'question of direct contact' (SE, 105). Connie (in *Lady C*), Ursula (in *The Rainbow*), and Lou (in *St Mawr*), in particular, are striving to be more alive. It is not 'meaning' they want, no, not at all. It is life – life and more life. 'The soul's first passion is for sheer life', Lawrence wrote in 'The Primal Passions', a poem (Poems I, 482). 'The only reason for living is being fully alive' (ib., 522). And again, in his "Return to Bestwood" piece, Lawrence states:

> I know that man cannot live by his own will alone. With his soul, he must search for the sources of the power of life. It is life we want. I know that where there is life, there is essential beauty. Genuine beauty, which fills the soul, is an indication of life, and genuine ugliness, which blasts the soul, is an indication of morbidity. – But prettiness is opposed to beauty. I know that, first and foremost, we must be sensitive to life and to its movements. If there is power, it must be sensitive power... What is alive, and open, and active, is good. All that makes for inertia, lifelessness, dreariness, is bad. This is the essence of morality. What we should live for is life and the beauty of aliveness, imagination, awareness, and contact. To be perfectly alive is to be immortal. (SP, 156-7)

D.H. Lawrence's urge to be alive is Nietzschean, as many critics have noted. Kingsley Widmer pointed out in "The Dialectics of Passion in Lawrence":

> It is... an exalted demand, religious in that sense. Acting by desire is often more arduous than is acting by ethical rule. As with the mysticism of the antinomian Christian – or the *arete* of the classical hero, or the *satori* of the Zen Buddhist – fulfilment of deep desires carries one necessarily outside the ordinary ethos and order – beyond good and evil in the Nietzschean sense. (in G. Salgado, 1988, 132)

Much of D.H. Lawrence's fiction is about the quest for new life. In *The Rainbow,* new life is in the Beyond. One must run to the Edge, and leap off, as Lawrence says in *The Crown* (P2, 374). Love is one way into new life. Each love-affair in *The Rainbow* is a beginning, a new life, a new birth (of Tom, for instance, on page 81). Later on in the novel Ursula makes the connection with religion: 'The Resurrection is to life, not to death' (326). Of course it is. Any resurrection must be to life and more life. A resurrection to death is useless. A resurrection and ascension into Heaven is understandable, because Heaven is often regarded as a new, bounteous life. Lawrence, in common with many dissatisfied, modern thinkers, claimed that Heaven must be on Earth, not elsewhere. Heaven must be now, not deferred bliss, but bliss now.

D.H. Lawrence: Infinite Sensual Violence

The three *Lady Chatterleys* chart the rebirth of a modern woman into new life. 'Life itself! Life itself! That was all that one could have, could yearn for!' (JTLJ, 114). Life is seen here as soft, quiet, deep. It is made up of simple things – presences felt, and quiet, dark thoughts, such as Elsa's experiences in the short story *The Overtone*: 'a silence of being' (CSS, 695).

※

The key to new life, to being more fully alive, is to develop a new relation, a new sense of touch with things. This is the thrust behind *Lady Chatterley's Lover,* the creation of a new sense of touch which Tommy Dukes yearns for and Connie Chatterley echoes: '"Give me the democracy of touch, the resurrection of the body!"' (LCL, 78). Also Hadrian, who is roused by Matilda touching his face in darkness in the short story *You Touched Me* (CSS, 376).

Touch, tenderness, contact – the yearning of *The Rainbow* is for something concrete, something definite, something real. *The Rainbow* is full of yearning, but, in the later works, D.H. Lawrence had a clearer idea what he and his characters were yearning for.

We've got to get into relation with things, asserted Lawrence a number of times. He meant a new, deep relation with the universe, with the body, and between men and women. The old ways are dead, as Ursula Brangwen (painfully) realizes. There must be new ways of living, and new relationships. I go along with that whole-heartedly.

The new relation must begin with the body. It must be physical (JTLJ, 265). The image of the new touch is Mary Magdalene touching the resurrected Christ (FCL, 85). *Touch me/ touch me not* – this saying from the *Gospels* fascinates D.H. Lawrence. He yearns for the right touch, not the cerebral one (Poems, 468). The body not the mind. The new touch must be holy, soft, of softly flowing blood (in the *Pansies* poems, ib, 471). In *Kangaroo,* Somers is struggling to 'make some kind of an opening' (77). The balance was uneven in the leadership novels of the 1920s, with their male protagonists in search of masters and power. Things changed in *The Plumed Serpent,* which has a female protagonist (although *The Plumed Serpent* is the most fascistic of Lawrence's novels).

D.H. Lawrence chose the (literary) novel as his battleground. In the novel he investigates ways of creating the new touch, and the new life. In the series of essays on the novel he is very optimistic. The novel, he claims, is the bright book of life, which can be full of the quick, not the dead. The novel is the highest art form. The great relationship, between man and woman, is best explored in the novel, he says

> ...the novel is a perfect medium for revealing to us the changing rainbow of our living relationships. The novel can help us to live, as nothing else can.

The novel is full of living people, full of livingness. The whole point of it all is to be fully alive, D.H. Lawrence says. Clearly he sees the novel as a *Bible*, as a modern, secular equivalent of the *Bible*. The *Bible* helped people to live in olden times, so the novel can do the same in our time. This is his general idea (SP, 165, 175, 177, 180, 185-8). Lawrence writes religious books, in which he hopes to reclaim the sacred in a secular world. Thus he sets love and holiness against the ugly, squalid world. There is the individual, full of love and yearning, and there is the hideous world outside. It's a pity, he says, that philosophy and fiction got separated (SP, 193). He wants both, both are necessary. So he put the religion, the philosophy, and the sacred back into secular fiction. The startling thing about Lawrence's books is that they take place in ugly, secular locations – the East Midlands, the horrible mining towns, the industrialized heartland of England – and yet they throb with life and religious fervour. It is astonishing that Lawrence does this, that he has such intense spiritual conflicts going on in such depressing and ghastly environments.

※

Wholeness is the goal. D.H. Lawrence gives it many names... *consummation, communion, transformation, oneness, blossoming*. Mystic wholeness is the goal of characters such as Ursula, Paul, Kate, Lou, and Connie. It means the enrichment of every area of life. It

means a transformation of body and soul into a richer kind of life, a
new beingness. 'How one must cherish the frail, precious buds of the
unknown life in one's soul' (Hux, 375). In the earlier works, wholeness,
oneness, unity, and totality was thought to be found in love. Paul
Morel describes it thus in *Sons and Lovers*:

> the real, real flame of feeling through another person... Something big and
> intense that changes you when you really come together with somebody
> else. It almost seems to fertilize your soul and makes it that you can go on
> and mature. (SL, 381)

Something 'big and intense' – this is what the lost girl, Alvina, also
wanted in *The Lost Girl* ('something serious and risky' [LG, 81]). Later
Lawrencean characters want something more than sexual consummation. They want something beyond love, beyond the individual – Lou,
Gudrun, and Kate. But D.H. Lawrence always kept his characters
yearning for something in people, in the man <—> woman relation.
He didn't know how to deal, really, with supra-personal love. It often
ends in death, or disillusionment (in *The Princess, The Plumed Serpent*,
etc). So it's better to restrict the yearning for wholeness to the man
<—> woman relation. For the characters who desire More Than This –
Lou yearning for wildness, for instance, in *St Mawr* – there is only
eternal disappointment. For Connie, in *Lady C,* one man, Mellors, is
enough. She will be faithful to Clifford (LCL, 312), but Mellors is her
true companion, her soul-mate. A key line appears at the end of
chapter 14 of *Lady Chatterley's Lover*: 'If only *he* would make her a
world' (222). It is a common dream: to escape from the ordinary world
and create a new one – through love. Jude and Sue in *Jude the Obscure*
try to do this and fail. In Thomas Hardy's fiction, the failure is society's
– it stems from enculturation, education, Christianity, marriage, laws,
government and materialism. In D.H. Lawrence's work the failures are
personal, within the self.

Middle period Lawrence saw consummation as a fusing of opposites
– the light and dark, the man and woman (P2, 375). The consumm-

ation took place in darkness. This is what Ursula Brangwen yearns for: 'she believed in an absolute surrender to love' (WL, 343). In *Twilight in Italy,* consummation can be non-human, uniting light and dark, being and non-being, in an ecstasy of transcendence (TI, 36-8).

Sex is usually the means to establishing wholeness. Blossoming is usually sexual in D.H. Lawrence's art. 'Blossoming means the establishing of a pure, new relationship with all the cosmos', he wrote in *Reflections On the Death of a Porcupine* (SP, 456-7). But in his fiction he usually sees blossoming in sexual terms. It occurs in people as sex. Thus the man in *The Escaped Cock*:

> He crouched to her, and he felt the blaze of his manhood and his power rise up in his loins, magnificent
> 'I am risen!' (CSN, 596)

Resurrection is sexual – the rising phallus equals the risen Christ. This melding of sex and religion, so vividly celebrated in Eric Gill's art, is still shocking to many people.

The delight of D.H. Lawrence's work is that he can be so simple – speaking of eggs hatching, of birds flying, of phallic erections, of flowers bursting open, of things blossoming. But sexual blossoming is limiting too. In many ways, *St Mawr* is a greater story than *The Escaped Cock* or *Lady Chatterley,* because the yearning there is supra-sexual, it goes beyond the self and the man<–>woman relation. *St Mawr* re-states the intense yearning for the Beyond found in *The Rainbow.* In that novel Ursula is the great yearner. In *Women In Love,* she is content with man–woman love and this is wrong, it is inauthentic to her character. Ursula is really like Lou, yearning for that extra wildness and wholeness beyond love, beyond humanity.

Seeds

> The things one cares about are all inside, like seeds in the ground in winter. But one has to attend to the things one only half cares about. And so life passes away. I expect it is always so, in the winter of our discontent, when the outside is mostly rather horrid and out of connection with the something that struggles inside. Luckily the inside thing corresponds with the inside thing in just a few people.
>
> D.H. Lawrence, letter, March, 1928 (in Huxley, 715)

Characters such as Ursula Brangwen in *The Rainbow* are all seed, quivering to find rich soil in which to settle and grow. In the poem 'First Morning', D.H. Lawrence adores growth – like André Gide, he speaks of mornings, of Spring, of flowers and eggs – all kinds of images of birth and growth (Gide often eulogized bright mornings in his *Journal*). In 'Spring Morning', Lawrence says:

> we are going to be summer – happy
> And summer kind (ib., 24)

It's impossible to grow in cities, so Lawrence's characters always need fields, wide-open spaces, dark woods and big skies. They need a rich soil in which to flourish. One of my favourite images in Lawrence's art is in *The Rainbow*, describing Will in the early days of his marriage to Anna:

> ...he was with her, as remote from the world as if the two of them were buried like a seed in darkness. Suddenly, like a chestnut falling out of a burr, he was shed naked and glistening on to a soft, fecund earth, leaving behind him the hard rind of worldly knowledge and experience. (R, 185)

So simple, yet so rich. It describes Will's state of being at this time, in easy-to-apprehend ways. Yet is also religious, recalling the scriptural notion of seeds falling on barren land, and also of the plant having to die so the seeds can be born. Life requires death so that more life can be born. And the aim is always for more life. 'What do we mean by higher? Strictly, we mean more alive. More vividly alive' (SP, 452).

The saddest thing is a seed that falls in the wrong place, at the wrong time. Many of Thomas Hardy's tragedies stem from this: Tess Durbeyfield grows with the wrong people (Alec d'Urberville), or the right people at the wrong time (Angel Clare). Jude Fawley thinks he needs Oxford to grow. Hardy's 1895 novel *Jude the Obscure* shows how wrong he is. Because bliss can happen anywhere, but all seeds need the right environment. The people in Lawrence's fiction are searching for that soft, dark space in which to develop. Some go to Mexico or Italia to find it. But it's not there. It's not in the external landscape, but in the soul, the self. You can find rich soil to grow in even in hideous places such as the English Midlands – Ursula grows there, and Connie does, too. The seed is you, the inside-you, and the rich, dark soil-space is also inside you. Sometimes it takes near-death for characters to realize this (Aaron, the princess, Gudrun).

※

Lawrencean rebirth comes from the inside, and the individual must desire it for herself. No one else can do her desiring for her. D.H. Lawrence is like the mediaeval troubadours in his attitudes towards desire. Sometimes he exalts it, at other times he despises it. Sexual desire is often a killer, a force of destruction (as in *The Princess, Women In Love* and *Sons and Lovers*). In the poem 'Lui et Elle' (from "Poetry of the Present"), he speaks of mutation, change, movement (Poems, 182-3). Consummation is for him sexual, and in flux. So he speaks of it as the meeting of two streams, two rivers of blood. Rivers, not wires or tubes or ropes. Not static images, but images of immense, endless movement.

> Desire itself is a pure thing... It is desire that makes the whole world living to me, keeps me in the flow connected. (P2, 455)

D.H. Lawrence is no happy Zen Buddhist, at peace with himself as he meditates in the lotus position. A mystic he may be, but he's one who can't keep still. He is a mystic on the move, and his mysticism is ever-changing. Because Lawrence is all desire, at times like André Gide or Arthur Rimbaud. He is drenched with desire, tormented by desire, like so many love-poets down the ages, from Sappho to Emily Dickinson. He is eternally dissatisfied. Eternal Existential angst and dissatisfaction is the hallmark of characters such as Paul, Ursula, Lou, Alvina, Aaron, Somers and Kate. They are not happy with what they've got at all. Some wandered around the world – Lou, Aaron, Somers, and Kate – while others wander within themselves (Ursula, Paul, Cyril, Daphne, Yvette, and Connie).

Like Thomas Hardy's characters, like most characters in literature – certainly in modern literature – D.H. Lawrence's people yearn and yearn. They are powered by desire.

> I think people ought to fulfil sacredly their desires... What we want is the fulfilment of our desires, down to the deepest and most spiritual desire... every desire, to the very deepest

wrote D.H. Lawrence (Hux, 360-1). Look inside your heart, said Lawrence: 'what do we find there? – a want, a need, a crying out, a divine discontent' (P2, 366). A divine discontent – the characters' response to it is sometimes disgust, as when Mrs Tuke in *The Lost Girl* says how disgusting it is when people cry out, 'Don't leave me!' (LG, 33). Connie goes utterly the other way. Like Ursula she is all yearning. She cries to herself:

> I want my heart to open! Oh, if only God or Satan, or a man or a woman or a child, or anybody, would help me to open my heart, because I can't do it myself! (JTLJ, 41)

This is the basic starting-point of so much of Western fiction. *Lady Chatterley's Lover* is a summary of all Western romances – the yearning, the binding up of politics and sex, the importance of the background and setting, the rival men, the saviour male coming to the rescue of the damsel in distress after the dragon has been slain. Connie is a classic fairy tale princess, a Sleeping Beauty waiting for her demon lover to 'awaken' her. She is the most Hardyan of D.H. Lawrence's women – she is so like Marty South or Tess Durbeyfield or Eustacia Vye. All that yearning, and not a man on the planet who can do anything about it.

5

Lady Chatterley's Lover

> *I am in a quandary about my novel,* Lady Chatterley's Lover. *It's what the world would call very improper. But you know it's not really improper – I always labour at the same thing, to make the sex relation valid and precious, instead of shameful. And this novel is the furtherest I've gone. To me it is beautiful and tender and frail as the naked self is, and I shrink very much even from having it typed.*
>
> D.H. Lawrence, April 12, 1927 (H. Moore, 972)

Lady Chattlerley's Lover (1928) is a great book in many ways. Yet it is not a unity: we can see how D.H. Lawrence pieced it all together. All the parts that go to make up the novel are exposed: we see how he creates his characters, his settings, his themes and his polemics. Often the bone structure of the book shows through the skilful skin of words woven around it. It's easy to see what Lawrence was trying to do.

The *story* is of the sexual awakening of Connie Chatterley at the hands of Oliver Mellors, but the *real* point of *Lady Chattlerley's Lover* is its cry for more tenderness in a savage and materialistic world. *This* is what it's 'about': tenderness, the purity of the loving touch, the sensual contact. What D.H. Lawrence (and Mellors) wants is a pure loving touch, that goes beyond language, and is totally nourishing.

D.H. Lawrence: Infinite Sensual Violence

Oliver Mellors is the mouthpiece of this philosophizing in *Lady C*, like Rupert Birkin in *Women In Love*. Yet most of the characters speak like Lorenzo: Connie, Clifford, Mrs Bolton, and Hilda – all of them spout Lawrencean metaphysics. The dialogues, as in the fiction of Lawrence Durrell or Thomas Hardy, are often impossible to believe. No one comes out with such stuff, with no pauses and no scripts! This is where the symbolism and philosophy outweighs the naturalism and the love relation.

Lady Chattlerley's Lover is a passionate plea for love between souls honest enough to open up to each other. 'It is a nice and tender phallic novel', said D.H. Lawrence, 'the last word, in all its meanings! – but very truly moral.' (Moore, 1033, 1046) Lawrence is brilliant in the passages of Mellors' speech. Mellors calls his philosophy 'cunt-awareness' and 'cunt-tenderness' (LCL, 256, 290). Mellors desires 'warm-hearted fucking'. The language is deliberate: to get to the root of the problem, to reclaim the basic words for the body and its ecstatic functions. So there is *cock, cunt, arse, shit* and *fucking*. Lawrence explains it thus in a letter to Lady Ottoline Morrell:

> ...I want, with *Lady C*, to make an adjustment in consciousness to the basic physical realities. I realize that one of the reasons why common people often keep – or kept – the natural glow of life, just warm life, longer than educated people, was because it was still possible for them to say fuck! or shit without either a shudder or a sensation. If a man had been able to say to you when you were young and in love: an' if tha shits, an' if tha pisses, I' glad, I shouldna want a woman who couldna shit nor piss – surely it would have been a liberation to you, and it would have helped to keep your heart warm. (December 28, 1928, Moore, 1111)

The revolution that D.H. Lawrence was aiming for in *Lady Chatterley* is indeed centred around language, and the perception and function of language. Sometimes the attempt comes across as affectation and self-conscious artifice, as when Mellors tries to impress Hilda by mentioning 'cunt an' tenderness' (256), or when Sir Malcolm says 'good bit of fucking' to Mellors in the club. This latter is truly awful dialogue which Lawrence should have altered. But he knew that '[f]or England, it is a very shocking novel: shocking!' (Moore, 1047). He was not bothered by sexual language, he claims: 'it isn't the names of things that bother me; nor even ideas about them.' (Hux, 55)

The so-called 'bad language' in *Lady Chatterley's Lover* is a problem, but then the whole book is an attempt to describe very deep emotions beyond words. And then there are the elements of chauvinism and pornography associated with words such as *fuck* and *cunt*. D.H. Lawrence's ambition can honesty justify the use of such words, *artistically*. He is trying to get to the heart of the business. Lawrence wanted to tackle the furtive, embarrassed discussion of sex so often found (still) in British and Western society. In his essay "The State of Funk", he wrote:

> And it was a long time before I was able to say to myself: I am *not* going to be ashamed of my sexual thoughts and desires, they are me myself, they are part of my life. I am going to accept myself sexually as I accept myself mentally and spiritually, and I know that I am one time one thing, one time another, but I am always myself. My sex is me as my mind is me, and nobody will make me feel shame about it. (SP, 369)

Interestingly, the word *fuck* in *Lady Chatterley's Lover* is introduced not by the gamekeeper Oliver Mellors, as one might expect (though he uses it by far the most), but by the group of intellectuals that surround Clifford towards the beginning of the book (35-39). Andrea Dworkin has used the words *fuck* and *cunt* many times in her fiction (in the novels *Ice and Fire* and *Mercy*). But she uses them as polemical, critical weapons within her (second wave) feminist discourse. Of Lawrence, Dworkin wrote in *Intercourse*:

> D.H. Lawrence tried to reinvent the use of so-called obscene words; he believed that the use of sexual euphemism created the dirty connotation of the more direct language... The *phallic reality* he intended was ecstatic, not dirty, a sacrament of fucking, human worship of a pure masculinity and a pure femininity embodied in, respectively, the penis and the cunt (another word favored by Lawrence). Lawrence himself was forced to recognize "how strong is the will in ordinary, vulgar people, to do dirt on sex" (201-2)

D.H. Lawrence: Infinite Sensual Violence

Andrea Dworkin's view is that these words can never be redeemed from pornography:

> words stay dirty because they express a contempt for women, or for women and sex, often synonyms, that is real, embedded in hostile practices that devalue and hurt women... Dirty words stay dirty because they express a hate for women as inferiors, that hate inextricably, it seems, part of sex – a hate for women's genitals, a hate for women's bodies, a hate for the insides of women in fucking. Dirty words stay dirty because they express a true dimension of women's inferiority, a forced inferiority, the dirty words part of the ongoing force; the penis itself signifying power over women, that power expressed most directly, most eloquently, in fucking women. Lawrence's *phallic reality* meant *power over,* and his "ordinary, vulgar people" had the same religion. Women stayed dirty because women stayed inferior. (*Intercourse*, 202)

(Ironically, Dworkin used those words herself in her fiction – thousands of them).

We see this power relation clearly in *Lady Chatterley's Lover,* where Mellors wields the 'obscene words' to gain 'power over' Connie, according to the second wave feminist view. She is subdued by his words, his penis, his aggression, his sexuality. Despite this power gaming (feminism is only one of 1,000s of ways of approaching a text), the sex scenes in *Lady C* are exquisitely described – and few writers can describe them like D.H. Lawrence. He has really freed up language here – unleashed it, recovered some of its raw power. The erotic language is both stylized and essential. Lawrence wants the experience to be transformative for Connie – that's why he uses tidal and oceanic imagery and metaphors. For Connie is transformed in the washes of her orgasms. The rippling, heaving motifs get as close to orgasmic bliss as anything else in modern, Western literature. The high point of the sexual prose is on page 258 of *Lady Chatterley's Lover,* when sex is used to burn out the soul, to go as deep as possible. Connie gets to 'the very heart of the jungle of herself'. The lovers embrace in a sharp, searing sensuality. This is marvellous. Here is real, fierce, burning sensuality, that is truly transformative.

In *Lady C,* sensuality is not sentimental tosh, or mere hedonism, but religious catharsis. After it, Connie is purified. The fire burns inside her, amid the heaving water of emotions, and she is made whole, made real. There is after this an 'ultimate nakedness', the kind of spiritual nakedness found in Robert Graves' late poetry. Absolute honesty, purity, totality. Here Lorenzo tries to describe going over the edge in sensuality, and he achieves his task more successfully than many previous authors. It is not a simple story, ballad-like, of a folkloric (sexual) awakening of a young woman by an older, rustic man. She has already enjoyed at least two sexual liaisons. This is something far greater, deeper, more poignant, more lasting. The sexual scenes in *Lady Chatterley's Lover* have been building up to this point, in which Connie, like a Sufi religious mystic (Rumi, Al-Hallaj, Jami), loses herself, and is purified by sheer sensuality, by the sheer fire of it all.

The sex scenes in *Lady Chatterley's Lover* must be flamboyant, over-the-top, as exuberant as possible, to show how extraordinary and beautiful will be the rebirth of the world through this kind of searing sensuality. These lovers destroy the world about them, like Anaïs Nin's lovers, to replace it with one of hot intimacy and the blind touch. 'Sex is so large and all-embracing that the religious passion itself is largely sexual,' asserted Lawrence in the essay "Making Love to Music" (SP, 400).

It is a phallic, not sexual, transformation. It is this for D.H. Lawrence because *life* sears through the lovers, not sex. Sex is used as the burning point of life (to paraphrase Joseph Campbell). Passion is the manifestation of the Lawrencean life-force. The power behind the phallus is life itself. The means are masculine – the phallus (not penis) is used in a mystical fashion: it brings religious awareness and magic. Religions need instruments; for Lawrence, the phallus is the instrument by which life is renewed. The phallus is a god, associated with Pan at the end of the book (315). It is an ithyphallic, pagan, burning religion he proposes. But it is a metaphorical and symbolic transformation, not a literal one. As in this quote from "A Propos of *Lady Chatterley's Lover*":

> Balance up the consciousness of the act, and the act itself. Get the two in harmony. It means having a proper reverence for sex, and a proper awe of the body's strange experience. It means being able to use the so-called obscene words because these are the natural part of the mind's consciousness of the body. (SP, 331)

D.H. Lawrence goes as far as language will take him, as far as he can take language. He cannot speak beyond this: hence the cathartic fire, the burning-up of soul and flesh. The struggle is realization, for the artist. Lawrence goes for the most difficult thing to realize in words: the touch of pure tenderness. It is not porn: Lawrence's goals are radically different from pornography (as Lawrence defines porn). Porno desires gratification, titillation, quick sex, always the tease: Lawrence cries out for tenderness, for intimacy and openness. 'Pornography is the attempt to insult sex, to do dirt on it,' he wrote in "Pornography and Obscenity" (SP, 312). The issue is confused by the use of the language of porn in *Lady Chatterley's Lover*. Lawrence is desperate: the language is a last, audacious attempt to describe the key Lawrencean relation, between man and woman.

Is porn all vile? some feminists have wondered. Nah, of course not. Porn is fantasy, in some views, and is thus of the same order as art, literature, theatre, or television, and its relation to actual, physical violence is controversial, and has been furiously debated in feminism. D.H. Lawrence tried to reclaim sex, to not be ashamed of it always, to integrate it into life. For the anti-censorship, pro-sex feminists, 'pornography is just about men and women enjoying sex together.' (Avedon Carol: "Snuff: Believing the Worst", in A. Assister, 129; see also Alison King, Gayle Rubin, Tuppy Owens, Claudia and Christobel MacKenzie in the same book.) As a counter-blast to the anti-porn feminists (of the Andrea Dworkin, Susan Griffin and Catherine MacKinnon ilk), anti-censorship feminists ask: is sex that bad, really? Why is *any* talk of sex instantly branded as 'wrong'? Therefore, why is porn, which depicts sex, automatically regarded 'bad' or 'wrong' or 'harmful'? Lawrence's position is that of a purist who wishes to remain faithful to his identity and desires: if a character desires sex, s/he says so, and follows her/ his desires, as Connie comes to do in *Lady Chatterley's Lover*.

D.H. Lawrence intellectualizes sex; his books are regarded as 'erotic', not 'pornographic' (this was part of the *Lady C* trial of 1960). His erotic art is not just high class, it is also seen as 'high art' or 'high culture', which raises it above mere, everyday porn. Another book that came out at the time of *Lady Chatterley's Lover* – 1928 – was Georges Bataille's *Story of the Eye,* which also tried to produce an intellectual, mystical, high art kind of pornography (though with different results):

> We slipped off all his clothes, and Simone crouched down and pissed on them like a bitch. Then she wanked and sucked the pig while I urinated in his nostrils. Finally, to top off this cold exaltation, I fucked Simone in the arse while she violently sucked his cock. (61)

It is a pity, and it's incorrect, even in terms of the sexual politics of D.H. Lawrence's novel, that it must still be the *man* who does the deed. Because Connie is forced to worship Mellors' penis. Yet here too Lorenzo goes for the heart of it all, for the symbolic-sexual core of Western patriarchy. The erect penis is among the most censored images in all of the Western world, and for good reason: to protect, in second wave feminist terms, the holy male lie. Lawrence exposes it, in comical scenes that teeter between misogyny and idiocy (in their effort to grasp at tenderness, lyricism and sexual love).

At the same time, Oliver Mellors does call his type of tenderness *cunt*-tenderness. That is, female power. Mellors recognises and acknowledges the feminine principle. He knows it; he exalts her body, again and again, in those wonderfully stupid pæans to her vulva, her ass, her body. He worships her body as the instrument of life, while she admires his will, his mind, his presence – and his penis.

Where D.H. Lawrence goes wrong is to have the female worshipping the male in the language and stance of the masculinity. Connie Chatterley worships Mellor's wiener by cooing over it, kneeling before him. This is a symbolic scene, sure, but Lorenzo simply doesn't have the capacity to create convincing female reactions and emotions here. Connie worships Mellors' pecker not as a grown woman but as an idiotic child, someone soft in the head. And the man is so flattered! Men are so easily pleased! Mellors demands total submissiveness from Connie after this ritual.

Few novelists have been so explicit. D.H. Lawrence has thrown out all the masks, all the colouring, all the soft descriptions, all the subtlety, and gone straight for the heart. Nothing must get in his way. Forget the niceties, he wants the truth, the real business. And he gets it. But it is so hot, so burning hot, so volatile, and so explosive, it's virtually untouched by British writers. Hence the debate, the scandal. It is Lawrence's honesty and total artistic integrity that just about pulls the book through. Even though *Lady Chatterley's Lover* can be demolished by feminists, Lawrence's plea for tenderness attempts to transcend all criticism.

There is no courtship: Mellors and Connie make love even without kissing first. In this respect, *Lady Chatterley's Lover* is modern – and bleak. The same happens in the film *Last Tango in Paris* (Bernardo Bertolucci, 1972). It is an anonymous love-making, a courtship of two lost souls, two people cast adrift, two egos alienated from their environments. Here is the bitter social criticism in the 1920s novel, with its emphasis on class, status, role, politics, and ideology. It is a hymn to the old world with its old ways. As with Thomas Hardy in his late novels *Tess of the d'Urbervilles* and *Jude the Obscure*, Bertie Lawrence laments the passing of tenderer times.

Unlike Thomas Hardy and most other novelists, D.H. Lawrence is brave enough to suggest something to go in its place (it's easy to criticize and demolish something, but *incredibly hard* to put forward new things). Here he scores. So many writers can carp on, hacking away at the socio-political structures of the Western world, but so few can actually suggest something worth living for, and none have the ability to outline a utopia in *clear, precise* detail.

But D.H. Lawrence *can* and *does* say what true living is. It is pure, sensual contact, the utter touch of love. The new touch, the new relationship. Connie is asked what it all is by Mellors: "'It's the courage of your own tenderness, that's what it is'" (290). This is a religious, Oriental stance (Buddha is invoked). Most of Lawrence's non-fiction prose grapples with the question of how to wake people up, to make them realize, to make them live. 'For man, the vast marvel is to be alive', he says in *Apocalypse* (110). (Admittedly, Lawrence's evocation of a utopian realm is pretty vague, but at least he has a go at it).

Each erotic meeting in *Lady Chatterley's Lover* is different, each sex scene gets more intense, generally, moving towards the orgasmic climax of the 'night of sensual passion'.

The first sexual scene in *Lady Chatterley's Lover* is soon over. The pleasure is all Mellors' pleasure: 'The orgasm was his, all his' (121). It begins with the blind instinctive caress as Mellors touches Connie's flank (120). He draws her into his gamekeeper's hut, and is in a hurry 'to enter the peace on earth of her soft, quiescent body' (120). Already D.H. Lawrence is describing sex in religious terms, having a woman is like experiencing peace on earth – like entering heaven. Supreme pleasure is sexual, but seen in a religious way.

This is how Oliver Mellors views sex: as a religious act, an act which re-establishes the Existential equilibrium on Earth, which encourages harmony and unity; which is a rebellious action, a kick in the eye of society. Throughout the 1920s book, D.H. Lawrence contrasts the secret, warm intimacy of the lovers and the mechanical, industrial world of society. The outside world is harsh and materialistic, while love, and particularly sex, offers a different way of living. Sex is in touch; society is out of touch. Lawrence thus far is saying nothing new here – the mediæval troubadours made the same point. Lovers since earliest times, in fact, must always have been aware of the huge difference between the shadowy intimacy of love and the bright exposure of the outside, everyday world.

The second time in *Lady Chatterley's Lover* that Connie and Mellors couple, Connie begins to awaken: 'Far down in her she felt a new stirring, a new nakedness emerging' (130). The third time they make out, the man is again eager in his lust. He wants her quickly, and leads her into some fir trees. The Lawrencean prose suddenly catches fire here, as Connie wakes up to experience:

> Rippling, rippling, rippling like a flapping overlapping of soft flames, soft as feathers, running to points of brilliance, exquisite, exquisite and melting her all molten inside. (138)

After this the relationship intensifies. D.H. Lawrence's prose becomes more focused. There are some marvellous pieces of description, as Lawrence tries to portray Connie's new state of being:

> Another self was alive in her, burning molten and soft in her womb and bowels… In her womb and bowels she was flowing and alive now… her womb, that had always been shut, had opened and filled with new life. (140)

We are used now to second wave feminist and third wave feminist writing of this kind, but for the time (1920s), it was a step forward – to have a male writer speaking of loving with the womb. The idea of the womb opening in love is marvellous, and rare in literature before D.H. Lawrence. He writes: 'His child was in all her veins, like a twilight' (143) – this is gorgeous.

During the next sexual encounter in *Lady C*, Connie Chatterley watches 'the ridiculous bouncing of the buttocks' (179). To her sex is ludicrous, or at least the male thrusting way of sex is stupid (that's the narrator stepping back to watch the tupping from a distance – and it's the way that sex's sometimes depicted in movies and TV). After this they make love again, and again it is his touch down her back that inflames her. Lawrence uses the age-old language of love, equating love with fire:

> She felt him like a flame of desire, yet tender, and she felt herself melting in the flame. She let herself go. (180)

D.H. Lawrence: Infinite Sensual Violence

D.H. Lawrence piles on the poetics, the descriptive words and the metaphors here, in the famous passage which describes Connie as an ocean: 'She was ocean rolling its dark, dumb mass'. Lawrence goes over the top here: 'she was deeper and deeper and deeper disclosed' (181). He ends the multi-orgasmic paragraph by writing:

> She was gone, she was not, and she was born a woman. (181)

Ouch! What a terrible line! Many people would dispute this: they might say that menstruation, if you insist on picking a physical/biological factor, marks the transformation from girl into woman – a transformation which does not require the male to make it happen, or to sanctify it. Or childbirth, another deeply transformative experience (again, largely a non-male experience). These are two women's mysteries Lawrence rarely describes; there are many others during adolescence. Instead, in *Lady Chatterley's Lover*, the birth of the woman occurs in heterosexual lovemaking – and only occurs with the plunging of the phallus. It is a feminine mystery valorized by the man, and his Ultimate Magical Tool. There are many ways to be reborn. It's a pity Lawrence thought the only one worth writing about was a sexual rebirth, dependent upon the man's member.

They make love for the fifth or so time in *Lady Chatterley's Lover* – after Connie has dutifully worshipped Mellors' penis – in the rain. Lovemaking in the rain! What a cliché! Yet it has to happen in this modernist, European re-run of every heterosexual love-affair in the history of the world.

The time after this is the culmination of the sex in the 1928 book, the 'night of sensual passion', Connie Chatterley's final and complete submission to the mystery and power of the phallus. A dildo wouldn't do, nor a vibrator, nor a sex toy – D.H. Lawrence hates clitoral sex, hates the idea of a woman satisfying herself sexually on her own. No, it takes a penis and a man to do it – and a vital man at that.

In *Lady C*, the last time they make love Connie commands him to kiss her womb (291) – the reverse of the phallus-worshipping ritual.

Mellors is scared – of bringing a child into the world. But there's never been a good time to bring children into the world. Every age has its full quota of pain, anxiety, danger and misery. What're you gonna do, wait ten thousand years? Until humanity is all cute and equal and peaceful? But Mellors realizes his mission on earth: 'to come into tender touch' (292). It is a Christ-like mission with him (of course it's Christ-like – he's a Lawrencen hero).

So much of *Lady Chatterley's Lover* blasts away at the hideousness of modern life. In this D.H. Lawrence is unsurpassed, unless by Samuel Beckett, in his violent denunciation of the modern world. He describes brilliantly the bland existence of mechanized, capitalist life, the urge to spend, spend, spend, to buy, buy, buy; the hateful nature of a machine-dominated world; the vapidity of the aristocracy; the stupidity of the masses; and the ineffectual nature of leaders and followers.

Here, D.H. Lawrence's fascist viewpoint rises up: he cannot disguise it. Here, in his politics, is he most awful of all. The sexism is transcended by the honesty and tenderness, but the fascism, which demands the death of wasteful people, is disgusting. Lawrence is a poet of extremes, but his reactionary politics is detestable at times. He is so often accurate and reasonable, but then he goes too far. Art and drama must exaggerate, granted, but the preaching becomes dogmatic. It should be left out. But Lawrence has to condemn the modern machine-world to make the new world of the lovers even more beautiful. It is simplistic, it is often ridiculously simplistic in its ideological vision. Lawrence is always dualistic. He's like Friedrich Nietzsche in his reductive worldview. We expect a little more complexity from such a visionary. But as he moves outwards, to the extremes of politics, Lawrence reduces his message to a simple cry for 'more life!', without really showing how it can be achieved beyond getting together with some juicy human body and trying out total tenderness:

> If England is to be regenerated... then it will be by the arising of a new blood-contact, a new touch, and a new marriage. (SP, 353)

D.H. Lawrence: Infinite Sensual Violence

Lady Chatterley's Lover is an uneasy mixture of elements: visionary politics and deep tenderness. D.H. Lawrence magical ability to present nature in its fullness is still there – the solitude, the presence, the silence of it all. The integration of the seasons with the love-affair is all too obvious, though. How the baby will be born in Spring, ready for their new life, and so on.

The characters, too, are ciphers for D.H. Lawrence's vision. They are heavily contrived and often clumsily manipulated. Connie is often bland, a vessel waiting to be filled by Mellors' masculine energy. She is not too assertive or independent. Her defiance of Clifford is mild. Mellors is aloof, and Connie has to do all the dirty work. The problem is that the ideals and visions are separated too often from the realistic characters. They are puppets of a novelistic demi-god. Sometimes it seems that Lawrence began with a message not a story. The form is not integrated so neatly with the content as it was in *The Rainbow*. Like *Jude the Obscure*, *Lady Chatterley's Lover* is a novel bursting with ideas, freighted with politics and comment. What gave *The Rainbow* its strength was the authenticity of its heroine, Ursula, as with Tess in *Tess of the d'Urbervilles*. The lovers in *Lady Chatterley's Lover* could be transported to a number of locations. The sense would change, but not too much.

Oliver Mellors proposes a sexual revolution, like his author. Not a feminist one, but a masculine intensification of heterosexual love-making. Mellors' ultimate act is the pure touch of total contact. But for Connie the ultimate act is sodomy. Connie, using second wave feminism, can be seen as a rape victim; she desires the degradation of buggery. But in D.H. Lawrence's work, anal sex is raised to a mystical stature. He makes sex mystical – he is the High Priest of Love, with sex as his God, and anal sex as the supreme, the most holy ritual, the holy of holies, the Holy Grail.

But the 1928 book is finally unconvincing in some ways, because too much value is place on sexuality. Sex is important, but not *that*

D.H. Lawrence: Infinite Sensual Violence

important, is it? Maybe it is. As Eugene Goodheart writes in *Desire and Its Discontents*:

> Religious rapture has often expressed itself through erotic language, subverting the ascetic strain in puritanical religion... In the failure of organized religion to provide fulfilment, eros becomes the "site" of the spiritual life, but its fulfilment more often than not turns out to be a terrifying experience. Lawrence half-discovered (I don't think he became fully cognizant of all that he imagined) that neither the sexual encounter nor the lover could bear the full weight of religious rapture. (65)

For Oliver Mellors, sex seems to be everything. Connie Chatterley goes along with it. But there is the baby, and all manner of things to contend with. Like Thomas Hardy, D.H. Lawrence stops his story before the birth of the child, before things get *really* difficult and complicated. In some ways, it's a cop-out. Mellors, and Lawrence, sidesteps many of the important issues facing the lovers. Sex alone can't carry the heavy religious, philosophical and Existential messages Lawrence wants to communicate. He wants to rejuvenate all of life, but something more than sex will be needed. There's more to life than tupping, but just what, Mellors can't really say. His idea of utopia is one in which men go around in tight, scarlet trousers that show off their butts. This image is like something out of a Hans Christian Andersen fairy tale filmed by Hollywood as a Technicolour musical of the 1950s. All the men dressed in tight, red tights! It is a strange fantasy – the fetish of someone who's eaten too much Hansel and Gretel gingerbread and sugar.

Full of memorable moments – the nude dancing in the rain, the extraordinary rippling orgasms, the inward silence of the trees – *Lady Chatterley's Lover* is nevertheless too aware of itself, too aware of its mission. It is the product of someone painfully self-conscious of his artistry. If only he could forget it all, and dive in! As he did with *The Rainbow*. *Lady Chatterley's Lover* is too self-aware, too much a jigsaw of elements that are not fully unified. A pity. The passion truly *sears*, but the authenticity is too often marred by preaching and whining. But

Lady Chatterley's Lover does fulfil its intentions – to explode a lovebomb in the minds of the British people. There D.H. Lawrence scores, as he always does. That's why he is probably our greatest novelist.

The First Lady Chatterley

This book (1926) is really a battle of class and social status and power-gaming, and money and materialism, and hereditary, and blood, not just a simple love-affair. All this is focused in the key dialogue scene in the book, on pages 177-184. Here Connie just wants the man, the lover. But Parkin (as Mellors was called) reckons he is not good enough – not a gentleman. He thinks she wants to make him into a gentleman. It is a class barrier. D.H. Lawrence cleverly talks of gentlemen and ladies. Connie can't express herself – "'I want you to be just a common man'", she says (179). Parkin of course takes offence to this, to the word 'common'. Who wants to be common, just average? So they can't say what they want to say – she wants a man, but a whole man.

It is depressing that this first version of *Lady Chatterley's Lover* revolves around sex, as much as the third *Lady Chatterley*. This would not have been D.H. Lawrence's last novel, though – he was working up to something far greater than this, one hopes – perhaps a mythic, sensual story in the manner of *The Escaped Cock*? Perhaps he might have moved into more fantastical areas, or maybe even written a big, sweeping series of books, like Lawrence Durrell's *Avignon Quintet*.

The style of *The First Lady Chatterley* is quite flat – there are few places where Lawrence really lets go. The love-scene under the moon is excellent (174), but almost a pastiche of *The Rainbow*. The piece on the phallus, blood and the masculine life-power is typical of Lorenzo, but fits in oddly amongst the otherwise pedestrian pastoralism.

D.H. Lawrence: Infinite Sensual Violence

But, even if *The First Lady Chatterley* had been written with the visionary prose and power of *The Rainbow*, it would still not be as good as that great book. The story is not strong enough; it is not believable enough; it doesn't have enough power behind it. Worse still are the characters – they're not as authentic as Ursula or Tom in *The Rainbow*. Parkin is not as rounded out as he is in the third version. And Connie, yearning though she is, never fully encourages our sympathy. She is held back – by the author, and by her self-awareness, her situation, her background. Ursula is fervent, like a Rimbaudian angel. Connie is heavy, soft, aching, but slow, somewhere between the quick and the dead.

The First Lady Chatterley is more political than the third version of *Lady C* – Parkin becomes secretary of the local government group, though the third version is more strident and intense in its political content. There is a long dialogue in *The First Lady Chatterley* about class difference which is not in the third variation. Duncan Forbes acts as a third party, someone Connie can talk to, a mere dramatic puppet, a catalyst for the action. A key statement occurs on page 248 of *The First Lady Chatterley,* telling us how Connie thinks that it is *relationship* which really counts: 'it was the new contact that was the clue to life.'

The first version of *Lady Chatterley*, then, contains only the germs of the last version. The characters, the plot, the tone and the vision changes. Phallic power only gets the odd mention (156). The passion is subdued. The love-making is hardly touched upon. The dreaded four-letter words occur (96, 127), but not much except in that awful last paragraph (253). The drama recalls Thomas Hardy, recalls Tess and Angel in *Tess of the d'Urbervilles,* and Sue and Jude in *Jude the Obscure,* the clash of working and middle classes. The classist conflict is a major issue in *The First Lady Chatterley*, holding the lovers back. Parkin is proud, unwilling to give in; Connie too has her pride but is willing to risk it all for a life with her lover. *The First Lady Chatterley*'s ending is awkward, a sudden tone of gloom and hatred from

Connie (246f) when she detects obscenity in everything. This sits oddly within the framework of the book.

John Thomas and Lady Jane

In many ways, this is the most satisfying of the three versions of the *Myth and Legend of Lady Constance Chatterley and Her Transformative Romance With a Gamekeeper.* It is more tranquil, more relaxed, more pastoral, more lyrical, more measured, and more drawn out than the other two versions. As Louise L. Martz writes in "The Second Lady Chatterley":

> It is as though Lawrence had asked himself: how would a novel in this English tradition have developed if George Eliot and Thomas Hardy had been able to present the explicit details of sexual experience and all the language that the common characters really would have used? (in G. Salgado, 1988, 107)

The Second Lady Chatterley, a.k.a. *John Thomas and Lady Jane* (1927), though, is not *Tess of the d'Urbervilles* or *Middlemarch* with 'fucks' and 'shits' added. If Tess had exclaimed to Angel, 'shit, Angel, I've never fuckin' trusted yer!', instead of, '"How silly I was in my happiness when I thought I could trust you always to love me!" (*Tess of the d'Urbervilles,* 417), the result would not be like any of the three *Lady Chatterleys*. Pastoral and 'English' though *John Thomas and Lady Jane* is, it is distinctly a Lawrencean product.

The phallic subtext in *John Thomas and Lady Jane* is vastly increased from book one, appearing on pages 282, 237f, 240, 310, etc. There is a big phallic tirade on page 237. D.H. Lawrence equates the rising of the phallus in erection with the risen Christ; the phallus is the true man (238); the phallus has its 'own weird godhead' (238); it has its 'own swarthy pride and surety, and 'fucking' went to the phallic roots of his soul.' Great stuff. Lawrence is thankfully otherwise quite restrained. Not often does he take over the narrative and start to stridently preach, as in the third version of *Lady Chatterley's Lover*. He gets on with the plot and narrative development. There are some wonderful passages in *John Thomas and Lady Jane*, such as on page 240 where he says:

> But he remained within the inner circle of the phallic angel, with the woman.

Here's the old, visionary D.H. Lawrence of *The Rainbow*, but also the preparation of the new, visionary stance of *The Escaped Cock*.

This phallic/ physical subtext is really well worked-out in *John Thomas and Lady Jane* – much better than in the first version. On page 173, D.H. Lawrence speaks of 'the goat-rhythm' of sex. In the following pages are some really lyrical, erotic passages.

The love-making in *John Thomas and Lady Jane* is often beautifully described – as in the rain (257), or the 'night of sensual passion' (276). The familiar D.H. Lawrence comes up with a wild orgasm of tolling bells (133) and the multiple dream of passion (136). There is much more lyricism in this book than in the other two versions of *Lady C*: of new life, and pure life (54, 114). Here Lawrence yearns for new life, for 'Life itself!' Lawrence talks about touch – of trees, of the earth, of hands and breasts (114). What a good, expansive mood he was in when he wrote this section.

And then Connie thrills too, to this new fresh 'democracy of touch'. This phrase, of Tommy Dukes' (69), is central to *John Thomas and Lady Jane*, but it is full of problems, because of its political overtones. D.H. Lawrence hates democracy – that averaging out of politics (in his essay "Democracy"). The phrase fuses the political and the personal, tenderness and the crowd. The book is full of such fusions, or attempts at fusion. *John Thomas and Lady Jane* is polemical, aching for a melding of politics and sexuality. It wants to make the individual, secret touch something vast and political, a system of interaction. This is the Grail of the novel – the Quest of it. The two lovers try to make it real. It starts off in a pastoral mode, moves beyond the erotic, and ends up cosmic. Connie equates Parkin's penis with the stars, saying it connects her to the stars (312).

Here D.H. Lawrence successfully blends the erotic and the political dimensions of the novel, fusing the dialectic with the dialogue on the class system (293), and marriage (301). It doesn't have the intensity of *The Rainbow,* but is softly extended. The yearning burns through, though – the yearning for new life, for passion, for touch, for tenderness. There are many good things in this book, much richness.

Such as: the snoozy sleep (186), the differences between London and Paris (282), or knowing and being (310). Or the descriptions of: the soft day (50), the sacred ground (101), mystery (125), the ugly Midlands (156), and the many pieces on flowers, trees, atmosphere and landscape. D.H. Lawrence is down at root-level here, his face pressed amongst the flowers, stems, ferns and leaves. He mentions, rightly, oak trees many times. *John Thomas and Lady Jane* is the product of someone awakening, which is ever the revelation in Lawrence's work, the mystery of him.

Connie is quieter than in *The First Lady Chatterley* or *Lady Chatterley's Lover,* but she is stronger, more sure of herself, in a way. She is the strong one in her union with Parkin. In the last version of *Lady C*, Mellors overwhelms her. Here in *John Thomas and Lady Jane,* she is powerful, and independent – closer to Ursula Brangwen. The later Connie is more like Alvina, the lost girl. Parkin, too, is a good character – believable, and rounded-out, and still something of a mystery.

The mechanism of *John Thomas and Lady Jane* is made all the more apparent because of the presence of the three versions. We can see which scenes D.H. Lawrence cut, which he enlarged, when comparing *John Thomas and Lady Jane* with the other two versions. The key scenes are still there, but extended. Some are the same, pretty much, while others are re-written to emphasize other points. You could make a long and exhaustive study of the differences between each version of *Lady* C. After all, D.H. Lawrence hardly ever wrote in series, unlike Marcel Proust or Anthony Powell. We have the two great novels, *The Rainbow* and *Women In Love*, as two parts of one work, and with this trilogy of *Lady Chatterleys*, the last great work.

6

The Escaped Cock

The whole thrust of *The Escaped Cock* (1928, also known as *The Man Who Died*) is towards the resurrection of the flesh. This is the message of *Lady Chatterley's Lover,* and it was an enduring obsession of D.H. Lawrence's: in December, 1914, he wrote 'we shall rise again in the flesh, you, I, as we are today, resurrected in the bodies' (Moore, 303). In "The Risen Lord" (1929), Lorenzo complains that the West has exalted the Crucifixion, not, as it should, the Resurrection. Easter, he says, is the beginning of the year, and it belongs to the joyous Resurrection. 'Christ risen in the flesh!... We must take the mystery in its fulness and in fact' (SP, 557). The apotheosis of being in the flesh is for Lawrence love-making. So:

> If Jesus rose as a full man, in full flesh and soul, then he rose to take a woman to himself, to live with her and to know the tenderness and blossoming of the twoness with her (CSN, 558).

This is the point of *The Escaped Cock* – the rebirth into life and love, the resurrection of the body and the senses: 'since I am risen, I love the beauty of life intensely', wrote D.H. Lawrence (ib., 560). A man is not whole without a woman, he says (Moore, 115). So he must have a woman.

D.H. Lawrence binds together many ideas in *The Escaped Cock*: Easter, sun, fire, blossoming, Spring, new life, the beginning of the year, dawn, the resurrected god (Christ, Osiris, Tammuz), eggs hatching, reawakening of sexuality, as well as the primal myths of the Western world. All the images are of rebirth.

The tomb is the womb, the egg in which 'the germ sleeps' (*Etruscan Places*, MM, 142). Christ is the phallus, dormant, waiting to rise. He is the seed, the germ, the bird waiting to hatch. He is Osiris, needing the tenderness of the woman (Isis) to bring him back to life, needing the nourishment of the womb.

The first part of the 1928 story deals with the man's reawakening to 'the astonishing place the phenomenal world is' (Moore, 975). 'It is for the Lord thus to rise', D.H. Lawrence wrote in "Resurrection" (P1, 737). The yearning is for a new touch, a new, tender touch to bring the soul and body back to life ('Ah, lay one little touch/ To start my heart afresh', said Lawrence in the poem 'Resurrection of the Flesh' (Poems, 738).

Christ is seen as a corn god, a fertility deity who must be sacrificed at Midsummer. Robert Briffault, Robert Graves and J.G. Frazer have written in detail of this myth. In D.H. Lawrence's hands, mythology becomes sexualized (inevitably). For the awakening is sexual. The crowning point of the story, just as the phallus is the crowning point, is the moment when Christ/ Osiris makes love with the priestess/ Isis:

> Himself bending over powerful and new like dawn.
>   He crouched to her, and he felt the blaze of his manhood, his power rise up in his loins, magnificent.
>   'I am risen!'
>   Magnificent, blazing indomitable in the depths of his loins, his own sun dawned and sent its fire running along his limbs, so that his face shone unconsciously.
>   He untied the string on the linen tunic, and slipped the garment down, till he saw the white glow of her white-gold breasts. And he touched them, and he felt his life go molten. – Father! he said, – why did you hide this from

me? – And he touched her with the poignancy of wonder, he said. – This is beyond prayer. – It was deep, interfold warmth, warmth living and penetrable, the woman, the heart of the rose! (CSN, 596)

Terrific prose this, rock solid, lucid and fresh. It begins with a Biblical simplicity – deeply poetic yet so simple and direct. 'I was brought up on the *Bible*, and seem to have it in my bones', Lawrence noted, like many authors in the West; 'language has a power of echoing a re-echoing in my conscious mind' (SP, 550).

The story of *The Escaped Cock* is written in this clear, Biblical style, such as in this quote from the *Gospel of John*:

Jesus saith unto her, Mary. She turneth herself, and saith unto him in Hebrew, Rabboni; which is to say, Master. Jesus saith unto her, Touch me not; for I am not yet ascended unto the Father... (20:16-17)

Occasionally, D.H. Lawrence departs from his simple, poetic, post-Biblical prose style, to produce phrases that appear nowhere in the *Bible*, such as 'the marvellous piercing transcendence of desire'. This is classic Lawrencean poesie, a prose style from the *Bible* treated with Symbolist over-indulgence, when simplicity becomes over rich. But in certain forms, such richness is justified – as in this sequence, which is the apotheosis of the story.

※

The Escaped Cock opens with the bird of the title escaping. As he leaves and squawks, he embodies the surge of life. The black and orange cock is the last in a line of many Lawrencean birds. In traditional symbolism, the cock is solar, a bird associated with courage, dawn, the Celtic underworld, and fertility, etc (J. Cooper, 38). The bird straining at the rope is one of the most potent images Lawrence created. It says it all. It perfectly expresses the need for a vivid, quick, phallic sense of life.

'What is actual living?' D.H. Lawrence asks in "Insouciance", composed about the time of *The Escaped Cock*: 'It is a question mostly of direct contact' (SE, 105). The cockerel's crow and the sunlight

D.H. Lawrence: Infinite Sensual Violence

reawaken the man who had died. Like the woman in the short story *Sun*, the man lies in the sun (CSN, 561).

The man is unusual among D.H. Lawrence's characters in *The Escaped Cock*, because he lacks desires (560). This is so unlike the people in *Women In Love* or *St Mawr*, who are a mass of conflicting desires and needs. Lawrence's Christ rises without desire. This is an important point, and over the next few pages Lawrence's narrator describes the desirelessness of the man. The state of non-desire is the being of the Buddha, of Oriental religion. But no Lawrence character can exist without desire, much as they might like to. Desire is woven into the Western soul at the deepest levels. Soon desire is awakened again in the man who died.

Primary colours are invoked in *The Escaped Cock* – the 'blue invisible', a black and orange cock, the green flame-tongues of the fig tree (562). The man who died has a white face and black eyes (558); the cock runs through the green of the olive and fig trees; the money is bright gold, like the sun (570); a 'black and white pigeon' flies out over the sea, another Lawrencean Holy Ghost (575); the Temple of Isis is pink, white and blue (577); the priestess is clad in yellow and white, like a narcissus flower (575). All these colours, which represent life in blood, contrast with the deathly grey of the man's clothing. He realizes that life is more powerful than death (563).

※

Like the man who loved islands, the man who died (in *The Escaped Cock*) wants to be utterly alone – '[f]or nothing is no marvellous as to be alone in the phenomenal world' (571). Cathcart too in *The Man Who Loved Islands* wants 'to make it [an island] a world of his own' (CSS, 671). Christ realizes that although there is the 'greater life' beyond the little individual life, he has risen for Woman (568). The struggle is between the desire for solitude and the yearning to be touched.

The dramatic thrust of *The Escaped Cock* pivots around the pure, tender touch (as in *Lady Chatterley's Lover*). For desire is like a flood – as it is described in *The Virgin and the Gipsy* (as a real flood), while in

D.H. Lawrence: Infinite Sensual Violence

The Rainbow it is a flood of horses:

> They came forth, these things and creatures of spring, glowing with desire...
> They came like crests of foam, out of the blue flood of the invisible desire...
> (562)

Christ cannot escape the waves of desire, soon he too is taken up by the flood.

The priestess of the Moon-Goddess in *The Escaped Cock* is waiting for the flood, for the phallic sun. She is waiting for the last piece of the jigsaw puzzle that is the god Osiris – his phallus. The man is the phallus, the missing link, the final clue that will replenish the womb, the lotus, the body of the priestess (578). D.H. Lawrence is here trading in the symbolism of the Frazer-Jung-Neumann-Graves-Eliade school. There are many parallels between *The Escaped Cock* and the mythic hero's return and his sexual initiation into the world of the Goddess (in Joseph Campbell's take on ancient mythology). The man who died brings Osiris's phallus, and, as in the ritual of the lance being plunged into the Grail or lake/ womb of Arthurian romances, he will regenerate the waste land inside us.

The Escaped Cock fuses the usual Lawrencean concerns, of sex and religion, flesh and spirit, where transformation is erotic. Kingsley Widmer writes in "The Dialectics of Passion in Lawrence":

> She [the priestess] searches rather for the mythical orgasms, the completion of and with an Osiris. For she is one of those 'rare women', a philosopher advised her, who waits 'for the re-born man'. In Lawrence's intentionally blasphemous transference of the Protestant conversion experience, and his outrageous punning on Christian sacramental language for eroticism, the virgin's lover can be no less than the scarred and sickly stranger, the post-crucifixion embittered Christ. Amoral sexual erection in place of spiritual resurrection is specifically based on his deceptively passing as the earlier dead-and-reborn deity. The eroticism may be summarised as piously slavish on the woman's part, anonymous, impersonal, religionist, overweening (images drawn from the ecstatic mystical tradition), a black-mass intercourse on an altar. (G. Salgado, 1988, 130)

D.H. Lawrence binds up many symbolisms and mythologies here – of

India especially, and Ancient Egypt, Greece, Sumer and so on. For instance, there is the tomb and the temple – the second cave and the womb of the priestess/ Goddess.

The new touch the priestess *The Escaped Cock* has in is 'farther than death' and the tenderness the touch brings is 'more terrible and lovely than... death' (583). But he loves the sun, and 'to touch her was like touching the sun' (591). Though a Moon-Goddess, the priestess is like the sun – she is with hot with life, exactly like the cock: 'How hot he is with life!' (572).

7

Sex and Death

Women In Love

Ash in the mouth throughout this classic book (completed in 1916, it was published in 1920), in the characters' mouths, after every scene, every meeting. Such a disgust, an antagonism, in this book. The characters bicker viciously. Such self-torture here. The characters squirm and convulse even at the most trivial of things. Birkin says something and Hermione writhes in agony. It's ridiculous. Everything is over-strained, on the point of collapse. The people seem to be in their death-throes. Many of the characters are pathetic – Hermione, and that stupid crowd at the Cafe – Possum, Halliday and co. How tiresome they all are, and how tiresome parts of the book can be. It's such a let-down after the ecstasies of *The Rainbow*. The blackness that lay in the hearts of the characters in *The Rainbow* has now become foregrounded, and the whole world is blackened, and tastes of ash.

 The battle between the sexes is at its most fierce in this 1920 book. All arguments are extended up to death. Things are not just bad, they're deathly. When something goes wrong, it's not painful, it means death. The men are death – both Birkin and Gerald are obsessed by it.

D.H. Lawrence: Infinite Sensual Violence

The novel plays out the age-old connection of love and death. The thing that connects them is sex. Sex and the body are the locations of the fierce duel between love and death. The book is decadent, and late, historically – it catches up on the French Symbolists, who in turn developed the decadent fantasies of the Marquis de Sade and Charles Baudelaire.

Sex, death, anality, excrement, war, violence, control – this is very much a novel about masculinist obsessions. It explores imaginative realms which for some feminists would be uncomfortably close to the masculinist domain of pornography. It is static, while *The Rainbow* is cyclic, in motion. *Women In Love* is full of restlessness, but this movement pivots around a single point, the meeting of men and women. *The Rainbow* moves through three generations, but *Women In Love* stays with one generation. It squashes everything together. And Lawrence splits up the protagonist, Ursula Brangwen, into two, the two sisters, and does likewise with the man. The result is the classic foursome, the Jungian quaternity, the earthly four of numerology. Forward motion is suspended in favour of an intense, spatial dialogue (the form is a musical theme and variations). The novel opens with a dialogue, getting right down to the metaphysics of sex.

Straight away the sexes are polarized. The women are seen together, in a sisterhood, in a female bonding. Later, D.H. Lawrence will note that when the sisters were together, they 'were quite complete in a perfect world of their own' (230). Men are not necessary. Worse, as Gudrun says, 'The man makes it impossible' (55). Two sisters and two brothers, the latter are later joined by a blood-oath and rite. It's all incest of the flesh here. Lawrence goes down to the most basic erotic fusion, which for him is not vaginal or of the womb, but anal. The anal connection is alchemical, Faustian, at the foundation of organic matter, beyond and below spirit, where atoms fuse and excrement turns into Freudian gold.

Gudrun is Ursula's wilder side. She takes over Ursula's fierce questioning characters in *The Rainbow*. For me this is a weakening of power, and makes *Women In Love* less effective than *The Rainbow*. Gudrun wants to know where to go (56); Ursula has already jumped, and Birkin acknowledges that Ursula has already 'burst into blossom' (186). Indeed, Ursula burst into blossom at the end of *The Rainbow*, but her troubles are not over yet. She fights violently with Birkin – he going for freedom, she for love (193). 'Birkin is consistently associated in the novel with images of death,' writes Daniel O'Hara in "The Power of Nothing in *Women In Love*":

> Lawrence has shown Ursula in transition from an idolisation of the ultimate vacancy of death to the radical critique of such idolisation when it is embodied for her in the person of Birkin. (156)

As the novel progresses, Rupert Birkin comes out with pure Lawrencean polemic – going beyond, lapsing out, becoming unconscious, etc (92-94). But he is all flux. To Gerald he says he wants the 'finality of love' with one woman (109-110). This is a death-of-God society. Without the woman there is nothing, 'seeing there's no God' (110). But later, to Ursula, Birkin talks of singleness and freedom, of going beyond love. Birkin is all change, and he is described visually as a lambent, quivering figure.

The men in *Women In Love* are associated with machinery, with death and despair (Gerald and the train, the mines, etc). D.H. Lawrence spoke of a sense of anguish as you approach London (113). He meant the mechanized, industrialized, gigantic modern city. Yes, that is part of any urban centre. But London is also the most exhilaratingly wonderful city on Earth.

The Goddess has been ousted from the man's world. The men go about naked in an unspoken but homoerotic way, while the Goddess is reduced to an ugly, primitive statue of a woman in labour (133). Birkin likes the finality of its sensuality, but Gerald is repelled by the Goddess statue. It's beyond him, something he cannot control.

As in *The Rainbow*, there are moments of intensity, of magic and ritual in *Women In Love* – when Gudrun watches Gerald dive into the lake, or when Hermione tries to kill Birkin, or when Gerald punishes the mare. Ursula and Birkin continue to have their debates on love and life. She asks, like Arthur Rimbaud, 'What am I doing here?' (208). Birkin brings in his concept of the star-equilibrium. Two five-pointed stars in contact, face-to-face. But men have an extra point, the phallus. And this is the cause of much of the conflict between the sexes.

All these tensions, between each couple, culminate in the chapter "Water-Party". Water is associated here with death. Gerald dives into the water in one of the first times Gudrun sees him – later he will walk into the frozen water of ice and snow in the mountains, to die; the Breadalby crowd go swimming; Gerald drops Gudrun's book in the water; Ursula and Birkin punt out to an island; then there is the long, excellent boat party chapter.

In bliss, the girls go off together, and the men come to find them. Gudrun dances, in another of D.H. Lawrence's great set-pieces, when he turns the energy up and writes brilliantly. Her dancing is wonderful – it is how Ursula should have reacted to the horses at the end of *The Rainbow*. Gudrun's dancing raises her above Gerald, while Birkin's strange shuffle perplexes Ursula (235). In this sequence, Lawrence brings together his four beings, and pushes them into focus. Each character is revealed in their attitude to love. Birkin is typically Lawrencean with his notion of the 'dark river of dissolution' (238), a different form of death to Gerald's, but to Ursula it's still death (there is a feeling that whatever Birkin suggested to Ursula – about anything – she would interpret as being linked to the Big Sleep).

Gerald is born again, in a deathly sleep, lapsing out for the first time ever (245), while Gudrun realizes her power over him. Then the death, the drowning, in the midst of life, and love, and pleasure, and only a few inches away. This is a terrific scene, one of those which D.H. Lawrence excels at. For he is still naturalistic, still within the bounds of the believable, and he is also psychologically true and heavily symbolic. Death *is* that close – there's the party-goers gossiping and laughing on the surface of the water, and it's all warmth and glowing light. Yet underneath is utter cold and blackness, another world altogether. This is a Beyond of Birkin's that is uninhabitable by humans. Even the King of Death, the Lord of the Underworld, Gerald, comes back from it exhausted and pale. This is a really wonderful scene, and it would be great with a single drowning. But Lawrence goes one better, and has a couple down there. It's crucial, and shows what could happen to the two couples of the novel if they venture into the waters of the unknown. For Gerald and Gudrun it would mean death, for Ursula and Birkin it means uncertainty. For Birkin hasn't yet fully worked out his new cult of life-beyond-love.

But the best thing about this sequence in *Women In Love* comes at the end of the chapter. It is Gerald who notices it: 'She killed him' (258). This image, of the entwined lovers at the bottom of the lake, focuses many of the symbols and themes of the novel: the couple, man and woman, death, water, darkness, and feminine soul-murder. *She killed him* – this could be more of Lawrence's uncertainty about women. But surely he's trying to say that you must love and take into account the whole of the woman, not just the material or sexual aspects. Gerald only sees the body and presence of Gudrun, the things he desires, and her power over him (something he greatly fears and resents), while Birkin only sees the beyond-self of Ursula, and denies her other sides. The point of the book is (partly) to show that much of love is projection, that the male projects onto the female what he desires, and that the female is eternally disappointed. The woman sees the whole man, from his body to his soul and all points in between. The man is partially blind, and only sees the parts he wishes to see. (The masochism, the emotional manipulation, and the passive-aggressive push-and-pull is clear to see in *Women In Love*. The masochism that underlies the Gudrun-Gerald relationship, for example, is something that Gerald refuses to acknowledge. The sadomasochism underneath the Ursula-Birkin relationship is also made obvious to the reader, though the characters pretend not to see it).

So much despair in this book, so much weariness, blackness and violence. But the frustration and despair these characters feel has no solution. Ursula, Birkin, Gerald and Gudrun are sinking down and down. Nothing can save them. Some of them – Gerald and Gudrun – don't want to be saved (Gerald commits suicide).

This is very much a modern novel. It is open. There is no linear thrust forward. The book wallows. The characters swerve from scene to scene, but they go in circles. The book could be 20 or 2,000 pages long. Each scene could be compressed, or expanded. Scenes could be added or taken away, with no great loss to the work. Because the point of the book – the evocation of weariness and despair – is there in every part of it, all the way through. The whole book is so tired, so weary. It is loose, and uneven. Uneven because sometimes D.H. Lawrence is coasting, then suddenly he works up his energy, and races forwards.

The trajectory of the book is towards death. Death in the midst of life. Death for characters who are just beginning to really live. They are in their 20s and 30s, at the height of their powers, yet they feel death all around them, all inside them. Not just in Gerald, but also in Ursula. She is dying, she thinks (260f). The despair of the age deeply affects her, this girl that was so full of life, so yearning for life and more life, in *The Rainbow*. Now she seems a shadow of her former self, just a foil for Birkin.

Death and darkness everywhere, then. Even when Ursula and Birkin make up after their bitter argument in 'Excurse', you can't believe they're happy. The despair is too deep. Their happiness is ephemeral. Joy in *Women In Love* is rare. *The Rainbow* is characterized by yearning – it is full of yearning. Everything is on the up. *Women In Love* is the opposite – everything is going down, sinking away, collapsing, fading, falling apart. The decay is everywhere – in the soul, in the families, in the relationships, in the towns, the work, the life.

Women In Love is all psychological – hardly any exterior scene-setting at all. It is so different from the conventional 19th century novel. The break with the past is complete. Hatred is the norm for much of the novel. How most of the characters *hate* each other! (267). Each character is arrogant, finding new ways and new reasons for hating the others.

The structure of the 1920 book is psychological – each section is structured around a conflict of minds: the four characters brought together in "Water-Party"; the two men in "Man to Man"; then Gerald and Gudrun in "Rabbit"; Ursula and Birkin in "Moony"; and the two men again in "Gladiatorial"; and the two women in "Woman to Woman" and so on.

So D.H. Lawrence has his characters studying the subject of the book – love, announced in the title – from a variety of angles. Love, or the death of love, stands like a statue at the heart of the book. The lovers walk around it, admiring it from a multitude of viewpoints. Lawrence Durrell will also do the same thing in his *The Alexandria Quartet*.

When Ursula and Gudrun are together they can transcend men and their yearning for them. But when Birkin and Gerald are together they are still yearning – Birkin for his star-equilibrium, and Gerald for something to alleviate his burden of boredom. Really all these characters are one. Birkin and Gerald are both death-obsessed, and they both drag their women into their deathly worlds. Ursula and Gudrun are the same, really – two sides of the same person. Gudrun merely takes on the rage of Ursula of *The Rainbow* era. The book could have been done using one person – an amalgam of Ursula, Birkin, Gudrun and Gerald. This single character could make love to itself, like a hermaphrodite, because that is what the people do anyway in *Women In Love*. They each make love to themselves. They project like mad, and get all upset when the other person doesn't conform to their mirror-image. How frustrated these babies get, when the mirror shatters, and real life lies behind it, and they realize that other people are not figments of their arrogant, wishful minds, but beings in their own right, entirely separate, with their own desires and needs.

The Goddess is dead – she drowned in the lake. Birkin hates the Goddess, hates domesticity, and bourgeois sex (269). He wants something beyond all that and is the most unhappy of the four. Gerald seems gloomy, but he is bored. When he gets something to do, he exults. He is much more easily pleased than Birkin. Gudrun is the most desperate of the four. Her dissatisfaction seems total. Ursula is the sanest, but she's picked someone very neurotic and unbalanced in Birkin.

The Birkin-Ursula romance pivots around religion and spirituality (the moon-shattering sequence in the chapter "Moony", the star-equilibrium, the marriage debate). The Gerald-Gudrun affair pivots around death, blood and violence (in "Rabbit" with the violent animal, torturing the mare and so on). Ursula and Birkin act out much of their emotional relationship in heated conversations, exchanges of bitter words rather than sweet kisses. This is from the "Moony" chapter:

> "How long have you been there?"
> "All the time. You won't throw any more stones, will you?"
> "I wanted to see if I could make it be quite gone off the pond," he said.
> "Yes, it was horrible, really. Why should you hate the moon? It hasn't done you any harm, has it?'
> 'Was it hate?' he said.
> And they were silent for a few minutes.
> 'When did you come back?' she said.
> 'To-day.'
> 'Why did you never write?'
> 'I could find nothing to say.'
> 'Why was there nothing to say?' (325)

And so on and on. Even in seemingly gentle exchanges like these there is much tension and angst.

✻

Ursula destroys Birkin in the chapter "Excurse", but not sexually, as she did with Anton in "The Bitterness of Ecstasy" chapter in *The Rainbow*, but verbally. She flattens him, calls him perverse and death-eating (389). Then comes the famous scene of bowels and loins being caressed. Dark floods of passion are released (always with the loins in Lawrence's fiction – no writer has ever used the word *loins* as much as Lorenzo!).

Some critics (such as Colin Wilson) have noted that this scene really consists of Ursula sucking Birkin's penis while she puts a finger inside his anus. But it's got to be more than oral sex with frills surely? D.H. Lawrence writes:

> She closed her hands over the full, rounded body of his loins, as he stooped over her, she seemed to touch the quick of the mystery of darkness that was bodily him. (396)

This is not just sex, not just a blowjob, otherwise D.H. Lawrence could have used the plain, crude style of pornography, and of some contemporary novels from Henry Miller to Charles Bukowski. Clearly Lawrence is going for something different here. It's not simply that he couldn't write *cock* and *cunt* in a novel published in 1920. He's aiming for a transcendence to a state of being beyond sex. Touch is the means, but the end is not orgasm, but transformation of being.

Sodomy and death and darkness are tied up together in D.H. Lawrence's work. He uses sodomy to get to the essence of things. For him, the essence is of the body, based in the body, before and after the spirit. A transformation that excludes the body is for Lawrence invalid. The body is the site of the mystery. So start with the body. Sex is one way of getting in touch with the body, but only one of many ways. The chief means is *touch* – pure touch. D.H. Lawrence is a priest of touch, not sex. The body is the site of mystery, religion, spirit. If Lawrence describes his characters at all, it is always as *bodies*, as presences, as flesh and blood. We always get a great sense of physicality in Lawrence's fiction, of people's physical bodies, their physical surroundings.

※

In *Women In Love,* the physicality is male. It's Women In Love we read of, but men's bodies we study. Women are decentred, psychologically. Birkin and Gerald are described fully, but Hermione's body is hardly evoked at all, and Ursula's and Gudrun's bodies are only described occasionally. We study men's bodies in detail, often through women's eyes. When Gerald stalks into Gudrun's house like a super-

D.H. Lawrence: Infinite Sensual Violence

natural being, his body dominates the scene. He moves from the deathbed of his father through darkness to the love-bed of his beloved. He feels transformed – it is ecstasy, a miracle, a marvel (430). But Gudrun lies awake, for hours. This is a superb piece of realization – the woman lying awake, holding her man who is in another world as the hours slide by (the scene occurs again in the *Lady Chatterley* books [John, 186]). The woman dies, inside, while the man replenishes himself in sleep. As Mary Daly writes in *Gyn/ Ecology* of Gudrun's state:

> ...it is the dull aching state of one who has sold her body and soul and will continue to do so. It is a state of perfectly false consciousness. (364)

Love-making in total darkness is a frequent occurrence in D.H. Lawrence's work. The soft twilights of *Sons and Lovers* and *The Rainbow* gradually become the total darknesses of *The Plumed Serpent*, *The Princess* and *The Ladybird*. Lawrence's landscapes become more extreme and the light in his landscapes gets more intense – it is a feature of Italy and Mexico. Lawrence's tendency is to go to extremes – to have full moons, or total darkness, or rushing rivers, or over-fertile peacocks, or savage mountains.

The chapter "Excurse" in *Women In Love* presents perhaps D.H. Lawrence's most concentrated description of sex. The emotions are fierce, tragic, painfully poignant. The language goes to extremes:

> Then a hot passion of tenderness for her filled his heart. he stood up and looked into her face. It was new and oh, so delicate in its luminous wonder and fear... "My love!" she cried, lifting her face and looking with frightened, gentle wonder of bliss... Kneeling on the hearth-rug before him, she put her arms round his loins, and put her face against his thighs. Riches! Riches! She was overwhelmed with a sense of a heavenful of riches. "We love each other," she said in delight... Her face was now one dazzle of released, golden light, as she looked up at him, and laid her hands full on his thighs, behind, as he stood before her. He looked down at her with a rich bright bow like a diadem above his eyes. She was beautiful as a new marvellous flower opened at his knees, a paradisal flower she was, beyond womanhood, such a flower of luminousness... She had established a rich new circuit, a new current of passional electric energy, between the two of them, released from the darkest poles of the body and established in perfect circuit. It was a dark

fire of electricity that rushed from him to her, and flooded them both with rich peace, satisfaction. "My love," she cried, lifting her face to him, her eyes, her mouth open in transport... It was a perfect passing away for both of them, and at the same time the most intolerable accession into being, the marvellous fullness of immediate gratification, overwhelming, outflooding from the source of the deepest life-force, the darkest, deepest, strangest life-source of the human body... (392-6)

In *Women In Love,* the Tyrolean, snowbound mountainscape is an extreme environment. The book has been full of darkness and nightmares, and D.H. Lawrence goes to the other extreme – all that snowy whiteness, which is deathly. It is not the pure, virginal white of traditional, Western culture, but the funereal white of Greece, Rome and the Orient – the colour of burial. White can also symbolize a birth into the new – something Gerald does not manage, as he goes to sleep in a white womb. Gudrun presides over Gerald's regression to the womb. She is the Scandinavian/ Teutonic Goddess of death, Freyja or Frigg.

The white mountainscape is the perfect location for the end of *Women In Love,* because it has been full of Northern angst and Gerald is like a Teutonic hero. If only the four had gone South, to Italy, to warmer climes. This is where Ursula and Birkin go, and rightly. But D.H. Lawrence took his fiction to extremes, and although his soul, and Ursula's, yearns for the Mediterranean, he halts his characters on the journey South in the mountains.

In the Gudrun-Gerald story, D.H. Lawrence uses the three symbolic colours of life, red, black and white. Red from the rabbit's blood, which unites Gerald and Gudrun in their deathly passion; black in the bedroom where they make love; white when Gerald dies.

Previously, D.H. Lawrence had used white for its positive life-affirming allusions – of holiness, purity, moon-power and childhood. Now, at the end of *Women In Love,* he reverses his sense of the poetic. *Women In Love* does mark the end of something important in Lawrence's work. After this the fire goes out of his art for some time. *The Lost Girl* is appalling, really, compared to *The Rainbow,* such a drop-down in intensity, skill and subtlety.

D.H. Lawrence: Infinite Sensual Violence

The 1920 novel ends unresolved. All the characters remain as they began – in turmoil. There is something beyond love and marriage – this is the debate of the book. But Birkin and Ursula haven't achieved it, and neither has Gudrun. Birkin's yearning for the extra relation with a man has come to nothing: 'it was intolerable, this possession at the hands of woman', says the narrator in Birkin-mode in the middle of the book (271).

Birkin's rejection of women's love, or, rather, his desire to transcend it, in favour of the blood brotherhood, is a great change, on one level, in D.H. Lawrence's art, and a change in bourgeois, Western fiction. Maria DiBattista writes (in *"Women In Love*: D.H. Lawrence's Judgment Book):

> Because marriage is disposed, by the sheer force of institutional inertia and by the reactionary demands of the "feminine" will to enforce a unity where none should exist, Birkin advocates the complementary, revolutionary relation of *Blutbruderschaft*. The truly subversive content of *Women In Love*, its well-conceived threat to the conventional attitudes toward human relationships propagated by the "bourgeois" novel, is in expanding the idea of spiritual mating to encompass a male-to-male relation, a broader and less interested relation than the "egoisme a deux" or "hunting in couples" (439) that characterizes modern marriages. (83-84)

In conventional drama characters are usually changed at the end of a play or a novel. In *Women In Love* there is no great change. Ursula seems no different: the characters are wearier, more cynical and more bitter. The war between love and solitude is not resolved, partly because D.H. Lawrence always sees things in terms of opposition, rather than two, complementary sides. Eugene Goodheart comments in *Desire and Its Discontents*:

> Lawrence opposes an ecstatic, onanistic aloneness (don't be deceived by his insistence that he is not alone) in which the self absorbs and is enhanced by the cosmos to the romantic cult of passion, the dissolution of the identities of lovers into a death-like unity. Lawrence discovers the terror at the heart of sexual passion. (78)

Birkin's questionings of heterosexual love race from one pole to the other, for Birkin is as reactionary as D.H. Lawrence. *Women In Love* rewrites heterosexual love, reaching a number of ambiguous conclusions that are not really conclusions. The novel remains 'open' to the end. It problematizes heterosexual love, and finds only a shaky fulfilment in homosexual brotherhood. The novel is apocalyptical, but not final.

8

Sex In D.H. Lawrence's Fiction

Sons and Lovers

Sons and Lovers (1913) is the first of the great D.H. Lawrence novels, though 1911's *The White Peacock* preceded it (he was 27 when *Sons and Lovers* was published in May, 1913). There is a finely detailed sense of space, of sacred spaces - such as the lamplit place where the kids play at night (116), and the many walks the lovers go on. Mother and son are linked in so many images and scenes - when they sleep together (107), when the boy brings home blackberries (108), when she brings back a bowl from the market (115). The Christmas preparations, as in *Aaron's Rod*, are marvellously described.

Paul Morel's first day at work is caustically invoked. If only D.H. Lawrence did this more often - it's great to see him laying into the harsh reality of things - the grubby stairs, the big interior of polished wood and decrepid, old furniture. These descriptions have a ring of authenticity about them, like the school rooms in *The Rainbow*.

The death of William clears the way for the mother-relation to become more intense. But at this point comes Miriam, an Arthurian Lady of the Lake. As in *The White Peacock*, the characters enjoy many moments of pastoral ecstasy (gazing at a jenny wren's nest, for example). Later, typically, when they become closer together, she wants to show him a 'certain wildrose bush' (209-210). This is a magical moment of communion, recalling that time in *Jude the Obscure* when Sue and Jude look at the roses at the fair. Almost every excursion features plants or flowers. The influence of Thomas Hardy is apparent here. D.H. Lawrence had read *Jude the Obscure* by December, 1910. Lawrence wrote this book twenty years after *Tess of the d'Urbervilles*, and there is a sense of continuity between the 19th century and the modern world.

Miriam and Paul both 'colour' or 'flush' or 'blush' as many times as Thomas Hardy's characters. How painful it all is! – to have these blushing people, flushing, so embarrassed, and often over really petty things.

Clara is introduced as a sexual force right from the start. D.H. Lawrence keeps mentioning her breasts, her neck, her hair, her body. She fascinates Paul, as much physically as mentally. She is described as magnificent, a real presence, an outsider. Her feminism, too, is really at odds with her mother, family and origins (320).

The chapter "Passion" in *Sons and Lovers* suddenly become breathless. Everything speeds up. The writing and pace accelerates. There is the long, typically Lawrencean scene as Paul drags Clara along the river. It is Paul who decides everything, who forces the issues. The mother fades from view as the two women in Paul's life take over (in the chapters "Defeat of Miriam", "Clara" and "The Test on Miriam"). Paul is so selfish. All of the novel focuses on him, and he imagines everything to pivot around him. As in *The Rainbow*, the combined weight of history, society, the family and the generations bear down upon one individual, the self-responsible soul.

Paul becomes the book. The second half of *Sons* is not nearly so good. The tension is lowered. It becomes the tale of a young man trying to assert himself sexually and socially. He loves and hates but only takes note of people when they're feeling or thinking about him. He does not really see Miriam as a person, nor Clara. He only hears them when they speak about him. He thinks Miriam adores him, for instance, and is shocked when he finds out she doesn't (359).

But Paul Morel is *not* D.H. Lawrence. The authorial presence is held back. Paul is allowed to destroy himself, to get swallowed by his own over-inflated ego. He talks about himself, he dominates Miriam and Clara. He is described very favourably – Clara loves him, his body, his quick movements. But there is something held back in her, something Paul cannot reach. Ditto Miriam – but her thoughts are not presented very well, or in any depth. Clara, too, only exists in *Sons and Lovers* for Paul. And Paul becomes arrogant, and blinkered. He drifts away from his mother (naturally) but also distances himself from the women in his life.

Clara is more of a mother-substitute. She is sexual, where Miriam is intellectual. Clara has motherly breasts – there Paul wishes to rest. The floral symbolism is immense, endless (see Chapter Two above). It is used right to the end – the mother sees sunflowers as she dies, and Paul shows her flowers. Love and death combine. There are many love and sex scenes. But they all orbit around Paul.

How tiresome he is! Going around spouting out his polemics, his feelings, his insecurities, his likes and dislikes, his grumbles. We weary of him. We don't want to hear him after a while. We don't want to watch him manipulate Miriam and Clara. How dismal is Paul's inability to deal with the flesh and blood monumentality of Clara, or the even intenser presence of Miriam. Miriam is right – Paul *is* a baby, but it's not good him blaming his mother. The mother, Paul thinks, comes between him and Miriam, because Miriam represents a spiritual and intellectual threat. Clara is motherly – always drawing him to her breasts. He desires comfort but, oh yes, he's in the real world, where people are moving in all sorts of directions, away from him, not just in his direction, orbiting around his ego. He must learn to live with frustration. He must learn what discrete ego boundaries are. His mother is of his flesh and blood. She dies – he weeps like a lover: "'oh my love!'" (469). However, to his credit, as soon as he's cried, "'oh my love!"' he goes downstairs and deals with details and plans.

The death of the mother in *Sons and Lovers* is long, protracted, and agonizing, as it should be. It goes on and on, and works very well. After it there is desuetude. Paul collapses. But he does not sink completely – he walks back to the town. He does not, like Gerald in *Women In Love*, walk out, following his death-drive.

The ending of *Sons and Lovers* is wonderful – the best in D.H. Lawrence's work, with *The Rainbow* and *St Mawr*. It is a full, satisfying ending. The book compares well with *Jude the Obscure*. Jude, like Paul, has two lovers. Clara, like Arabella, is all body – she, too, has comforting, motherly breasts. She is associated with materialism and the work ethic – she sews for a living and works in Jordan's factory. Arabella too is very materialistic. It is the passion of the body, of the earth, of labour and people-power.

Miriam is like *Jude the Obscure*'s Sue Bridehead – all soul, religious and intense. Higher up, they yearn to do something great in the world. They demand much of their men, Clara too wants a man, a real man – but a dignified, whole, earthy human being. Baxter has more self-honesty than Paul.

For Miriam, as for Sue in *Jude the Obscure*, the spiritual union is enough. Both women are so close, intellectually, to their men. But their men ache for sex – ache for it while also feeling repulsed by it. They, the men, are the deficient ones. Yet Paul constantly projects his fears, guilts and desires onto Miriam. It is Paul, not Miriam, who is intense. Miriam is transcendent. Her aching for the religious life is transcendent, yet it aims to go into and transform the world.

Paul Morel, meanwhile, is impotent. He cannot transform things, least of all himself. D.H. Lawrence shows this clearly in Paul's art. It has been said that *Sons and Lovers* is a portrait of the artist as a young man (G.M. Hyde, 30). It is not: its main theme is love, or male-female emotions and relations, in relation to parents and mother-love.

Paul's art is negligible. It is something he does to amuse himself. It fits in with his mother's home life and control of the home. Paul does not push his art along: it is a very minor theme. Only by the end of the novel do we believe that Paul could *maybe* become something of an artist. Up until then, no. His art is vaguely defined. It is blurred, unimportant. It is something the character does in the lulls between the real action and stuff of the book, the love-relationships.

Miriam is individual: she desires union. Paul wants Lawrencean separateness. Clara is Woman embodied. But she cannot be a Muse. Miriam is a Muse – Paul must not cheapen or weaken this Muse-bond by the sexual act. Ancient themes.

The deficiency is in Paul, but the book is (nearly) always from his viewpoint. We get caught up in Paul: we get claustrophic. We do not see Clara or Miriam on their own often. But Clara escapes Paul, and goes back to Baxter (a Phillotson character from *Jude the Obscure*), and Miriam too escapes.

D.H. Lawrence has inverted Thomas Hardy's *Jude the Obscure*: the spiritual woman gets the hero first, then comes the sexual initiation. It is too late for Paul; all his beliefs about people have been shattered or have become dogmas.

"'Mother!'" he cries, in the wilderness – an outsider, an outcast, a stranger in his homeland, ostracized by himself. Tied still to the mother, by the umbilical cord of his own devotion, he cannot break free. Even in death the cord is still tight, coiling like a Serpent-Goddess around him.

Sons and Lovers is a great novel. The first part is weighty, full, simple yet rich. The last third deteriorates; the narrative collapses into a bunch of dialogues and meditations of self-absorption.

D.H. Lawrence: Infinite Sensual Violence

The Plumed Serpent

In *The Plumed Serpent* (1926), the heroine, Kate, being female, helps to position the exploration of gender, power and difference: it really brings out the masculine themes of brotherhood, violence and phallicism. Ursula Brangwen would really hate this barbaric world, while Kate desires much of it. The masculine imagery is powerful – the sperm-like lake, the phallic cacti, the many dark-faced, black-eyed men. Splitting the Quetzalcoatl cult up into two men, Ramon the shaman, and Cipriano the general, is also a good idea. These men seem believable. They come alive, as Kangaroo or Struthers never really did. Lilly (in *Aaron's Rod*), too, is indistinct in comparison.

But Ramon is possibly D.H. Lawrence's most fully evoked *man* – he is, like Mellors in *Lady Chatterley's Lover*, the heavily sensual figure. It is always his body that is described. His loins, his bare chest, but not his feelings. Ramon is the culmination of the Native Americans in *St Mawr* and *The Woman Who Rode Away*, the gipsy in *The Virgin and the Gipsy*, and Gerald in *Women In Love*: the phallic man, the phallic angel. This is as much a sexual as a religious novel. The story relates the establishment of a religious cult, but it is just as much the story of a woman's search for Something More Than Men, more than love, more than religion, more than life. For Jean-Luc Godard, *The Plumed Serpent* 'is the most important novel of the twentieth century'.

Kate yearns in *The Plumed Serpent*, and only partially gets what she's yearning for. Cipriano cannot deliver; Ramon could, but he is not committed to love, nor to her. He wants only the re-establishment of the old cult of the Snake-God.

The consummation in the tale is religious, of the ego, the yearning self, not sexual, but spiritual. There is a sexual union, between Kate and Cipriano. D.H. Lawrence turns up the pace and the words here, as they make love: she with her beak-like, clitoral Aphrodite sex, and he makes her open up, all hot and wet (459f). Lawrence's distrust of powerful, 'cocksure' or phallic women manifests itself here, and always seems ridiculous. In the battle between matriarchy and patriarchy in Lawrence's fiction, matriarchy *seems* to win, but phallic patriarchy remains ascendant. As Sandra M. Gilbert writes in "Potent Griselda: "The Ladybird" and the Great Mother":

> in the complex of late works constituted by *The Escaped Cock, Lady Chatterley's Lover,* and *Etruscan Places*, he affirms matriarchal authority more humbly than ever before while definitively creating the only theology that he can imagine to oppose it: the religion of the phallus. (153)

Sun

With *St Mawr*, *Sun* is D.H. Lawrence's most accomplished story of a woman's yearning for otherness and wildness. *Sun* is a visionary tale of purification and regeneration, centring around a sun ritual. The colours, symbols (snake, sun, flame, nudity), setting and language fuse to create a powerful exaltation of phallic energy:

> She slid off all her clothes and lay naked in the sun, and as she lay she looked up through her fingers at the central sun, his blue pulsing roundness, whose outer edges streamed brilliance. Pulsing with marvellous blue, and olive, and streaming white fire from his edges, the sun! He faced down to her with his look of blue fire, and enveloped her breasts, and her face, her throat, her tired belly, her knees, her thighs and her feet. (CSS, 495)

The sensualism is total, and though the source is called phallic and male, the transformation is of feminine power. The last image is of a child in the womb – the fruit of her sun-god worship:

> Ripe now, and brown-rosy all over with the sun, and with a heart like a fallen rose, she had wanted to go down to the hot, shy peasant and bear his child. (508)

D.H. Lawrence: Infinite Sensual Violence

The initiation in *Sun* is into the phallic mystery, as Kate found out in *The Plumed Serpent* (347, 463). D.H. Lawrence has long clung to this philosophy, of the phallus. In *Twilight in Italy,* an early work, he wrote: 'The phallus is a symbol of creative divinity' (TI, 68).

Here, in *Sun*, the woman is able to keep the two energies in harmony – womb and phallus, yin and yang, female and male. But when the balance is upset, the result is disaster. There are three short stories that are very violent. The violence is phallic, sanctified by holy, male brotherhoods, and ritualized patriarchically. *The Princess, The Woman Who Rode Away* and *None of That* are the three stories, alternatives to *The Plumed Serpent.*

The Woman Who Rode Away

The Woman Who Rode Away begins where *St Mawr* left off. The woman is eternally dissatisfied – with her life, husband, house, kids, etc. She goes in search of the old gods of the Native Americans, in the Sierre Madre, Mexico.

The woman is already dead – she admits it (515). As in *The Princess,* the journey into the mountains is meticulously and lovingly described. She accepts everything that happens to her ('The woman was powerless', 518). She is numb, like the wife in Paul Bowles' *The Sheltering Sky.* The men manipulate her, strip her, keep her prisoner. She watches their dances, hears their mumbo-jumbo. Her apotheosis is to be the Winter sacrifice. The narrator describes it in naturalistic, and magical, terms. But in reality it is a gang-rape. The story is claustrophic, uncompromising, deadening. Despite the important elements of the story – the symbolic death, the yearning for sacrifice – its structure (a group of men and one woman) is irredeemably chauvinist. It exalts patriarchy, and victimizes women. The woman's yearning to be sacrificed is itself largely a patriarchal construct, and one that should have been examined in this story. Instead, Lawrence goes too far, he cannot remain impartial. Instead of emotional exorcism the story produces ideological violence; and the relationship between the sexes (here portrayed cartoon-style as the sun and moon, page 532), is smashed to pieces.

The Virgin and the Gipsy

The Virgin and the Gipsy is, oddly, an orthodox and weak tale, compared to the rest of late D.H. Lawrence fiction. It is composed in a jaded, ironic storyteller's tone. The gipsy embodies otherness for the heroine Yvette, like the horse in *St Mawr*, or like Mellors in *Lady Chatterley's Lover*. The tale is rather mediocre and tame, but Lawrence does let himself go towards the end, with the big set-piece, the flood (a reworking of *The Rainbow*). This is life, and sexuality, overtaking Yvette. Lawrence makes this clear: he writes:

> She was barely conscious: as if the flood was in her soul. (CSN, 544)

The flood is also a narrative device to get Yvette and the gipsy close together, in a small space. They're chastely but sensuously united – the scene recalls *The Horse-Dealer's Daughter*. And Yvette does get a kind of apotheosis. But despite the vivid and merciless depictions of the hideous, old Granny and slavish Aunt, the writing is too loose, too ill-defined, written at half-power.

D.H. Lawrence: Infinite Sensual Violence

St Mawr

St Mawr is one of D.H. Lawrence's most accomplished works: the formal elements – of language, character and structure – are fully realized; the prose style is Lawrence at his best; the symbolism is spot-on and merged fully with the narrative; the philosophic discourse is rich and powerful, tactile yet intangible, fierce yet ambiguous.

Love and men are not enough for the heroine, Lou. She wants, like Ursula in *The Rainbow*, something bigger than that. The tale is full of spiritual yearning, for Something More Than This, something more than the Western, bourgeois way of life. The horse symbolizes the wildness that Lou yearns for. The descriptions of the horse are among the most potent, the most tantalizing, the most deeply-felt scenes in Lawrence's work:

> For some reason the sight of him, his power, his alive, alert intensity, his unyieldingness, made her want to cry... But now, as if that mysterious fire of the horse's body had split some rock in her, she went home and hid herself in her room, and just cried. The wild, brilliant, alert head of St Mawr seemed to look at her out of another world... Why did he seem to her like some living background, into which she wanted to retreat? When he reared his head and neighed from his deep chest, like deep wind-bells resounding, she seemed to hear the echoes of another, darker, more spacious, more dangerous, more splendid world than ours, that was beyond her. And there she wanted to go. (CSN, 287, 299)

No male human can live up to St Mawr the horse. The horse is a gigantic, mythical being, imbued with as much magic and phallicism as D.H. Lawrence can muster. Lou gets close to her yearned-for wild land. The horse takes her from London, to the borderlands of Wales, and to New Mexico. Each location is beautifully evoked. On the ride in Shropshire, the 'old savage England', is reclaimed (CSN, 335). The search continues; it is often bleak, full of dissatisfaction. Where is the human equivalent of St Mawr the horse? Nowhere – men are tame boys (322, 326, 362), with no wildness, no Pan in them anymore, if there was any in the first place. Only Lewis and Phoenix have a little of the horse's pagan magnificence.

With such a great welling up of restlessness in the mother and daughter in *St Mawr*, there can be no easy ending to the tale. There is nowhere for such restlessness to go. The story is wide open – Lou's wonderful speech on wildness shows that the savage pilgrimage will continue. The horse renders the story concrete and believable. Like the escaped cock, the horse works on a number of levels, and is far more fulfilling as a symbol than the phallus in *Lady Chatterley's Lover*.

'It would be terrible if the horse in us died for ever, as he seems to have died in Europe,' D.H. Lawrence wrote in January, 1924 (Moore, 769). In Lou, the spirit still thrives. Rather than ending on the bleak, nihilistic note of *The Woman Who Rode Away, None of That* or *The Princess, St Mawr* ends on a terrifically powerful and positive note. Lou says:

> "Now I'm here. Now I am where I want to be: with the spirit that wants me... And I am here, right deep in America, where there's a wild spirit wants me, a wild spirit more than men. And it doesn't want to save me either. It needs me. It craves for me. And to it my sex is deep and sacred, deeper than I am, with a deep nature aware deep down of my sex." (CSN, 427)

9

Conclusion

D.H. Lawrence is still widely discussed by critics because his art is challenging, on a number of levels. Writers such as Henry Miller, Anaïs Nin, Melvyn Bragg, Raymond Carver, Tennessee Williams and Lawrence Durrell invoke his name because he is the epitome of passion. He is the creative artist who never stopped creating, who worked heroically, like Vincent van Gogh or J.M.W. Turner, non-stop, right to the end. He was full of conviction. His views kept changing, but he believed in them passionately. He was an honest artist, an intuitive seer, the working-class boy from the sticks who made good, who aimed as high as possible, who came closer than most to achieving his goal.

Critically, D.H. Lawrence is a celebrated modernist, championed by such important critics as F.R. Leavis. But Lawrence can be approached in all sorts of ways critically, as the many books and papers on him show. Like Joyce and Woolf, he is one of the key modernists. He draws together discussions on politics, religion, philosophy, sexuality, language and a host of other topics. His popularity as a subject of criticism must be due to this multivalence – the way Lawrence engages so many aspects of contemporary culture. The range of his investigations was large. He can be taken to task in so many areas.

He is still on the shelves in bookstores and libraries, next to T.E.

D.H. Lawrence: Infinite Sensual Violence

Lawrence, F.R. Leavis, Doris Lessing and R.D. Laing on the 'L' shelf.

Why is D.H. Lawrence so popular, still read so much? Well, like Thomas Hardy, he provides strong stories, rich in discourses on sexuality, struggle, the family and character. Like Shakespeare, D.H. Lawrence's tales have a momentum, a pace and a strength of narrative which pulls the reader along. He is a hypnotic writer, and his books are enjoyable to read. He is not deliberately difficult, or pretentious. He deals, like Greek tragedy, in timeless themes – of love, being, death.

His books also flatter the bourgeois reading public's values, like Jane Austen's or Arnold Bennett's books. The reader can pass over the controversial issues raised in the texts (such as the cult of religious transformation through sodomy), and concentrate on the story and characters. Lawrence's characters range from proletariat to aristocracy. Thomas Hardy, in novels such as *The Woodlanders*, created hierarchies of characters – working class people (Marty South), the bourgeoisie (Grace and Fitzpiers) and the upper classes (Mrs Charmond). D.H. Lawrence creates similar characters and hierarchies, although both he and Hardy are uncomfortable with upper class figures. Where they both score (as also writers such as Albert Camus and André Gide), is when they depict people who struggle with work, familial relations, sexuality, loneliness and yearning. At this level, in the depiction of people trying to live and love, Lawrence is brilliant, as good as any other novelist. And it is the fiction, particularly the novels, which lie at the heart of Lawrence's achievement and popularity.

Lawrence is still read primarily because he is a brilliant writer of fiction. And, if you want it, he adds religious, political, ideological investigations into the modern human condition.

D.H. Lawrence's fiction is alive. It is not dead simply because it is pre-postmodern, or because it is a century old. Francesco Petrarch is still relevant, still fresh, as is Petronius or Homer. The same problems – of love and death – still beset people today. Lawrence's fiction is alive and kicking still because it does address vital, ever-recurring issues. But also because some of the contemporary issues (contemporary to the

1920s) are still with us today: such as the ugliness of modern towns and the hideousness of machine-like labour.

Another reason for D.H. Lawrence's popularity is possibly the many extra-diegetic elements in his stories: the religion of love, the cult of sexuality, the sacred body, the river of blood, the societal criticism, etc. Lawrence does have many strange ideas – or ideas that have been a part of the philosophical underbelly of Western culture (found in Gnosticism, the troubadours and courtly love, numerology, mediaeval bestiaries, symbolism, etc).

D.H. Lawrence's notions – his peculiar sense of physiology, for instance (embodied for me in words such as *loins*) – are not so much strange as strangely (and passionately) expressed. It is the sheer force and energy of Lawrence's communication that makes him fascinating. While other artists might um and er about sexuality, Lawrence dives right in, and says what he thinks, in a powerful manner.

Then there is his prose, which is remarkably lucid. His phrasing is not awkward, as Thomas Hardy's sometimes was. He does not use difficult words, as Bertrand Russell or Aldous Huxley did. He is not obscure, like James Joyce or Samuel Beckett. One of Lawrence's chief æsthetic tactics is musical repetition (which also makes him sometimes tiresome to read). He uses simple mechanisms of prose – comparisons, colourful adjectives, vivid verbs and metaphors. His innovation was to somehow describe subtle, inner states of being by using simple, everyday words (such as *darkness, touch, strange*). 'Darkness' is an ordinary word, describing something that covers half the planet. Yet in Lawrence's hands it becomes a powerful way of describing a state of being. If you write 'she walked home through the darkness', you have a simple statement. But if you write 'the darkness was inside her as she walked', you have a psychological insight; action has become emotion. This is Lawrence's realm, where naturalism becomes symbolism, realism becomes emotionalism and politics becomes psychology.

Plus, it must be said, that D.H. Lawrence is fascinating as a personality in himself. His life was intriguing – the many travels, the famous people he mixed with (Bertrand Russell, Aldous Huxley, Katherine Mansfield, Richard Aldington, Lady Ottoline Morrell, etc), the crazy ideas (of never-to-be utopias, for instance).

D.H. Lawrence's life and personality adds charisma and weight to his art, as with Vincent van Gogh, Arthur Rimbaud and Lord Byron. But his colourful personas do not cheapen his art, nor take away from the fact that he was a marvellous writer.

Bibliography

All books are published in London, England, unless otherwise stated.
Abbreviations appear after each entry

D. H. Lawrence

FICTION, POETRY

The White Peacock, Penguin, London, 1982/7 [WP]
Sons and Lovers, ed. K. Sagar, Penguin, London, 1981/6 [SL]
The Rainbow, ed. J. Worthen, Penguin, London, 1981/6 [R]
Women in Love, ed. C.L. Ross, Penguin, London, 1982/6 [WL]
Aaron's Rod, Penguin, London, 1950 [AR]
The Lost Girl, Penguin, London, 1950 [LG]
The Lost Girl, ed. J. Worthen, Cambridge University Press, Cambridge, 1981
The Boy in the Bush, ed. P. Eggert, Cambridge University Press, Cambridge, 1990
Kangaroo, Penguin, London, 1950 [K]
Kangaroo, ed. B. Steele, Cambridge University Press, Cambridge, 1994
The Plumed Serpent, ed. R.G. Walker, Penguin, London, 1983/5 [PS]
The First Lady Chatterley, Penguin, London, 1973 [FLC]
John Thomas and Lady Jane, Penguin, London, 1973 [JTLJ]
Lady Chatterley's Lover, Penguin, London, 1960 [LCL]
Lady Chatterley's Lover, ed. J. Lyon, Penguin, London, 1990
Lady Chatterley's Lover and *A Propos of Lady Chatterley's Lover*, ed. M. Black, Cambridge University Press, Cambridge, 1993
Mr Noon, ed. L. Valsey, Cambridge University Press, Cambridge, 1984

The Trespasser, Penguin, London, 1960
Selected Short Stories, ed. B. Finney, Penguin, London, 1982/5
Collected Short Stories, Heinemann, London, 1974 [CSS]
The Complete Short Novels, eds. K. Sagar & M. Partridge, Penguin, London, 1982/7 [CSN]
The Complete Poems, eds. V. de Sola Pinto & W. Roberts, 2 vols, Heinemann, London, 1972 [Poems]
Poems, ed. K. Sagar, Penguin, London, 1986
The Symbolic Meaning, ed. A. Arnold, Viking, NY, 1964
The Portable D.H. Lawrence, ed. D. Trilling, Viking, London, 1947

ESSAYS, TRAVEL

Phoenix: The Posthumous Papers, ed. E. Macdonald, Heinemann, London, 1956 [P1]
Phoenix II: Uncollected, Unpublished and Other Prose Works, eds. W. Roberts & H.T. Moore, Heinemann, London, 1968 [P2]
A Selection from Phoenix, ed. A.A.H. Inglis, Penguin, London, 1971 [SP]
Study of Thomas Hardy and Other Essays, ed. B. Steele, Cambridge University Press, Cambridge, 1985 [TH]
Movements in European History, Cambridge University Press, Cambridge, 1989
Reflections On the Death of a Porcupine and Other Essays, ed. M. Herbert, Cambridge University Press, Cambridge, 1988
Selected Essays, Penguin, London, 1950 [SE]
Selected Literary Criticism, ed. A. Beal, Heinemann, London, 1967 [SLC]
Fantasia of the Unconscious and Psychoanalysis of the Unconscious, Heinemann, London, 1961 [F]
Apocalypse, ed. M. Kalnins, Granada, London, 1981 [A]
Apocalypse, ed. M. Kalnins, Cambridge University Press, Cambridge, 1979
Mornings in Mexico and Etruscan Places, Penguin, London, 1960 [MM]
Sketches of Etruscan Places and Other Italian Essays, ed. S. de Filippis, Cambridge University Press, Cambridge, 1992
Twilight in Italy, Penguin, London, 1960 [TI]
Twilight in Italy and Other Essays, ed. P. Eggert, Cambridge University Press, Cambridge, 1994
Sea and Sardinia, Seltzer, NY, 1921
D.H. Lawrence and Italy, Penguin, London, 1985

LETTERS

The Collected Letters of D.H. Lawrence, ed. H.T. Moore, 2 vols, Heinemann, London, 1962 [Moore]
The Letters of D.H. Lawrence, ed. A. Huxley, Heinemann, London, 1934 [Hux]
The Letters of D.H. Lawrence, ed. J. Boulton, Cambridge University Press, Cambridge, 1979- [Let]

Lawrence in Love, ed. J. Boulton, University of Nottingham, 1968
D.H. Lawrence's Letters to Bertrand Russell, Gotham Book Mart, NY, 1948
Letters of D.H. Lawrence and Amy Lowell, Black Sparrow, Santa Rosa, 1985
The Quest For Rananim, ed. G. Zytaruk, McGill-Queen's University Press, Montreal, 1970
Letters From D.H. Lawrence to Martin Secker, Bridgefoot, Iver, Bucks., 1970
The Centaur Letters, University of Texas at Austin, TX, 1970
Letters to Thomas and Adele Seltzer, Santa Barbara, CA, 1976
"D.H. Lawrence and Frieda Lawrence: Letters to Dorothy Brett", *D.H. Lawrence Review*, 9, Spring, 1976

Others

T.H. Adamowski. "*The Rainbow* and Otherness", *D.H. Lawrence Review*, 7, Spring, 1974
—. "Being Perfect: Lawrence, Sartre and *Women in Love*", *Critical Inquiry*, 2, 1975
R.M. Adams. *After Joyce*, Oxford University Press, NY, 1977
D. Albright. *Personality and Impersonality: Lawrence, Woolf and Mann*, University of Chicago Press, 1978
John Alcorn. *The Nature Novel from Hardy to Lawrence*, Macmillan 1973
Richard Aldington. *Portrait of a Genius, But...*, Reader's Union/ Heinemann 1951
Keith Alldritt. *The Visual Imagination of D.H. Lawrence*, Arnold 1977
W.T. Andrews. *Critics on D.H. Lawrence: Readings In Literary Criticism*, Allen & Unwin 1971
A. Armin. *D.H. Lawrence and America*, Linden Press, London, 1958
—. *D.H. Lawrence and German Literature*, Heinemann, London, 1963
A. Arnold. *D.H. Lawrence and America*, Linden, London, 1958
C. Asquith. *Diaries*, Hutchinson, London, 1968
Alison Assister & Avedon Carol, eds. *Bad Girls and Dirty Pictures: The Challenge to Reclaim Feminism*, Pluto Press 1993
A.M. Aylwin, ed. *Notes on D.H. Lawrence's The Rainbow*, Methuen 1977
John Atkins. *Sex in Literature: the erotic impulse in literature*, Panther 1972
Peter Balbert. *D.H. Lawrence and the Psychology of Rhythm: The Meaning of Form in The Rainbow*, Mouton, The Hague 1974
—. & Philip L. Marcus, eds. *D.H. Lawrence: A Centenary Consideration*, Cornell University Press, Ithaca, New York 1985
—. "The Loving of Lady Chatterley: D.H. Lawrence and the Phallic Imagination", in Partlow & Moore, eds, 143-158
—. "Forging and Feminism: *Sons and Lovers* and the Phallic Imagination", *D.H.

Lawrence Review, 11, 1978, 93-113
J. Barron. *D.H. Lawrence: Feminist Readings*, London, 1992
G. Bataille. *Literature and Evil*, Calder & Boyars, London, 1973
—. *The Story of the Eye*, Penguin, London, 1982
A. Beal. *D.H. Lawrence*, Oliver & Boyd, NY, 1961
M. Beeb, ed. *Modern Fiction Studies, D.H. Lawrence number*, 5, 1, Spring, 1959
M. Bell. *D.H. Lawrence: Language and Being*, Cambridge University Press, Cambridge, 1991
Catherine Belsey. *Critical Practice*, Routledge 1980
Gabriel Ben-Ephraim. *The Moon's Dominion: Narrative Dichotomy and Female Dominance in Lawrence's Earlier Novels,* Associated University Presses, New Jersey 1981
Leo Bersani. *A Future For Astynanax*, Marion Boyars 1978
R. Beynon, ed. *D.H. Lawrence*, Icon, Cambridge, 1997
M. Black. *The Literature of Fidelity*, Chatto, London, 1975
—. *D.H. Lawrence: The Early Fiction*, Macmillan, London, 1986
—. *D.H. Lawrence: The Early Philosophical Works*, Macmillan, London, 1991
L. Blanchard. "Love and Power", *Modern Fiction Studies*, 21, 3, 1975
—. "Women Look at Lady Chatterley: Feminine Views of the Novel", in *D.H. Lawrence Review*, 11, Autumn, 1978
—. "Lawrence, Foucault, and the Language of Sexuality (*Lady Chatterley's Lover*)", in P. Widdowson, 1992
Haskell M. Bloch & Herman Salinger, eds. *The Creative Vision: Modern European Writers*, Grove Press, New York 1960
Harold Bloom, ed. *D.H. Lawrence's The Rainbow*, Chelsea House Publishers, New York 1988
—. ed. *D.H. Lawrence's Women in Love*, Chelsea House Publishers, NY, 1988
A. Brandabur. "The Ritual Corn Harvest Scene in *The Rainbow*", *D.H. Lawrence Review*, 6, 1973
E. & A. Brewster. *D.H. Lawrence*, Secker, London, 1934
Derek Britton. *Lady Chatterley: The Making of the Novel*, Unwin Hyman 1988
Keith Brown, ed. *Rethinking Lawrence*, Open University Press, Milton Keynes 1990
M. Brunsdale. *The German Effect on D.H. Lawrence and His Works*, Peter Lang, Las Vegas, 1978
Anthony Burgess. *Flame Into Being: The Life and Work of D.H. Lawrence*, Heinemann 1985
W. Bynner. *Journey With Genius*, Day, NY, 1951
Philip Callow. *Son and Lover: The Young D.H. Lawrence*, Stein & Day, New York 1975
Joseph Campbell. *The Power of Myth,* with Bill Moyers, ed. Betty Sue Flowers, Doubleday, New York 1988
—. *This business of the gods*, Windrose Films, Ontario, Canada 1988
Catherine Carswell. *The Savage Pilgrimage: A Narrative of D.H. Lawrence*, Cambridge University Press 1981
F. Carter. *D.H. Lawrence and the Body Mystical*, Archer, London, 1932

David Cavitch. *D.H. Lawrence and the New World*, Oxford University Press, New York 1969
Jessie Chambers. *D.H. Lawrence: A Personal Record*, Cambridge University Press 1980
Maurice Charney. *Sexual Fiction*, Methuen 1981
Tom Chetwynd. *A Dictionary of Symbols*, Collins 1982
P. Christensen. "Problems of Characterization in D.H. Lawrence's *The Rainbow*", AUMLA, 77, May, 1992
Colin Clarke. *River of Dissolution: D.H. Lawrence and English Romanticism*, Routledge and Kegan Paul 1969
—. ed. *D.H. Lawrence: 'The Rainbow' and 'Women In Love': A Casebook*, Macmillan 1969
D. Consolo, ed. *D.H. Lawrence: The Rocking Horse Winner*, Merril, Columbus, 1969
H. Coombes, ed. *D.H. Lawrence: A Critical Anthology*, Penguin 1973
A. Cooper, ed. *D.H. Lawrence*, D. H. Lawrence Society, Nottingham, 1985
J.C. Cooper, *An Illustrated Dictionary of Traditional Symbols*, Thames & Hudson, London, 1978
H. Corke. *Lawrence Apocalypse*, Heinemann, London, 1933
—. *Neutral Ground*, Barker, 1933
—. *D.H. Lawrence*, University of Texas Press, Austin, 1965
—. *In Our Infancy*, Cambridge University Press, Cambridge, 1975
E. Cornwell. "The Sex Mysticism of D.H. Lawrence", in *The Still Point*, Rutgers, 1962
J.C. Cowan. *D.H. Lawrence's America Journey*, London, 1970
—. *D.H. Lawrence: An Annotated Bibliography of Writings About Him*, Northern Illinois University Press, De Kalb, 1985
—. *D.H. Lawrence and the Trembling Balance*, Penn State University Press, 1990
Gail Cunningham. *The New Woman and the Victorian Novel*, Macmillan 1978
I. Cura-Sazdanic. *D.H. Lawrence as Critic*, Manoharlai, Delhi, 1969
Keith Cushman. "D.H. Lawrence at Work: "The Shadow in the Rose Garden"", *The D.H. Lawrence Review*, 8, 1973, 32-46
—. "Virgin and the Gipsy and the Lady and the Gamekeeper", in Michael Squires, op.cit., 154-169
—. & Dennis Jackson, eds. *D.H. Lawrence's Literary Inheritors*, Macmillan 1991
H.M. Daleski. *The Forked Flame: A Study of D.H. Lawrence*, 1968
Mary Daly. *Pure Lust: Elemental Feminist Philosophy*, Women's Press 1984
—. *Beyond God the Father*, Women's Press 1985
—. *Gyn/Ecology: The Metaethics of Radical Feminism*, Women's Press, 1979
R. Darroch. *D.H. Lawrence in Australia*, Macmillan, Melbourne, 1981
R. Davis. "The Mother As Destroyer: Psychic Division in the Writings of D.H. Lawrence", *D.H. Lawrence Review*, 13, 1980
Paul Delany. *D.H. Lawrence's Nightmare: The Writer and His Circle in the Years of the Great War*, Basic, New York 1978
Emile Delavenay. *D.H. Lawrence: The Man and His Work: The Formative*

Years, 1885-1919, tr. Katherine M. Delavenay, Southern Illinois University Press, Carbondale 1972
—. *D.H. Lawrence and Edward Carpenter: A Study in Edwardian Transition*, Taplinger, New York 1971
Maria DiBattista. "*Women In Love*: D.H. Lawrence's Judgment Book", in P. Balbert, 1985, 67-90
J. Diski. *Nothing Natural*, Minerva, 1990
Carol Dix. *D.H. Lawrence and Women*, Macmillan 1990
G. Doherty. "Death and the Rhetoric of Representation in D.H. Lawrence's *Women in Love*", *Mosaic*, 27, 1, 1994
R. Drain. *Tradition and D.H. Lawrence*, Groningen, 1960
J. Dollimore. *Sexual Dissidence*, Oxford University Press, Oxford, 1991
G. Donaldson. "Men in Love?", in M. Kalnins, 1986
H.D. *Bid Me To Live*, Grove Press, NY, 1984
R. Drain. *Tradition and D.H. Lawrence*, Groningen, 1960
R.D. Draper. *D.H. Lawrence*, Twayne, 1964
—. *D.H. Lawrence: The Critical Heritage*, Routledge & Kegan Paul, London, 1970
—. "The Defeat of Feminism", *Studies in Short Fiction*, 3, 1966
—. "*The Rainbow*", *Critical Quarterly*, 20, 3, 1978
—. ed. *D.H. Lawrence: The Critical Heritage*, Barnes & Noble, NY, 1979
Andrea Dworkin. *Intercourse*, Arrow 1988
—. *Letters From a War Zone: Writings 1976-1987*, Secker & Warburg, 1988
—. *Pornography: Men Possessing Women*, Women's Press 1984
—. *Right-Wing Women*, Women's Press, 1983
Roger Ebbatson. *Lawrence and the Nature Tradition*, Harvester Press, Brighton 1980
—. *The Evolutionary Self: Hardy, Forster, Lawrence*, Barnes & Noble, NY, 1982
Duane Edwards. *The Rainbow: A Search for New Life*, Twayne/ G.K. Hall, Boston 1990
A. Efron, ed. *Paunch*, D.H. Lawrence number, 26, April, 1966
S. Eisenstein. *Boarding the Ship of Death: D.H. Lawrence's Quester Heroes*, Mouton, The Hague, 1974
Mircea Eliade. *Ordeal by Labyrinth*, University of Chicago Press 1984
—. *A History of Religious Ideas*, I, Collins 1979
David Ellis & Howard Mills. *D.H. Lawrence's Non-Fiction: Art, Thought and Genre*, Cambridge University Press, 1988
—. *D.H. Lawrence: The Dying Game, 1922-30*, Cambridge University Press, Cambridge, 1998
E. Engelberg. "Escape From the Circles of Experience: D.H. Lawrence's *The Rainbow* as a Modern *Buildungsroman*", *PMLA*, 78, March, 1963
T.L. Erskine, ed. *Literature/ Film Quarterly*, D.H. Lawrence number, 1, 1, January, 1973
Julius Evola. *The Metaphysics of Sex*, East-West Publications 1985
J. Farr, ed. *20th Century Interpretations of 'Sons and Lovers'*, Prentice-Hall, 1970
E. Fay. *Lorenzo in Search of the Sun*, Vision, London, 1955

E. Feinstein. *Lawrence's Women: The Intimate Life of D.H. Lawrence*, HarperCollins, London, 1993
–. "Portrait of a marriage", *The Sunday Times*, 18 Sept, 1994
–. *Lady Chatterley's Confession*, Macmillan, London, 1995
John Ferguson. *An Illustrated Encyclopaedia of Mysticism*, Thames & Hudson 1976
A. Fernihough. *D.H. Lawrence*, Clarendon Press, 1993
M.L. Fielding, ed. *Notes on D.H. Lawrence's Sons and Lovers*, Methuen 1975
P. Firchow. "Rico and Julia: The Hilda Doolittle – D.H. Lawrence Affair Reconsidered", *Journal of Modern Literature*, 8, 1980
G.H. Ford. *Double Measure: D.H. Lawrence*, Rinehart & Winston, NY, 1965
J. Foster. *D.H. Lawrence in Taos*, University of New Mexico Press, Albuquerque, 1972
M. Freeman. *D.H. Lawrence*, University of Florida Press, 1955
Alan Friedman. *The Turn of the Novel*, Oxford University Press 1966
L.B. Gamache. "The Making of an Ugly Technocrat: *The Rainbow*", *Mosaic*, 12, 1978
R. Garcia & J. Karabatsos, eds. *A Concordance to the Short Fiction of D.H. Lawrence*, University of Nebraska Press, 1972
Sandra M. Gilbert. "Potent Griselda: "The Ladybird" and the Great Mother", in P. Balbert, 1985, eds, 130-161
E. Gill. *Beauty Looks After Herself*, Sheed & Ward 1933
–. *Autobiography*, Cape 1940
–. *Last Essays*, Cape 1942
–. *The Letters of Eric Gill*, ed. W. Shewring, Cape 1947
S. Gill. "The Composite World: Two Versions of *Lady Chatterley's Lover*", *Essays in Criticism*, 21, 1971
S.L. Goldberg. "*The Rainbow*", *Essays in Criticism*, 11, 1961
A. Gomme, ed. *D.H. Lawrence*, Harvester Press, 1978
E. Goodheart. *The Utopian Vision of D.H. Lawrence*, University of Chicago Press, 1963
–. *Desire and Its Discontents*, Columbia University Press, NY, 1991
D. Gordon. *D.H. Lawrence as a Literary Critic*, Yale University Press, 1966
–. "Sex and Language in D.H. Lawrence", *20th Century Literature*, 27, 4, 1981
Robert Graves. *The White Goddess*, Faber 1961
–. *Mammon and the Black Goddess*, Cassell 1965
E. Green. "Schopenhauer and D.H. Lawrence on Sex and Love", *D.H. Lawrence Review*, 8, 3, 1975
Martin Green. *The Von Richthofen Sisters: The Triumphant and the Tragic Modes of Love*, Basic, New York 1974
H. Gregory. *Pilgrim of the Apocalypse*, Grove, NY, 1957
L. Greiff. *D.H. Lawrence: 50 Years On Film*, Southern Illinois University Press, 2001
E. Grosz. *Sexual Subversions*, Allen & Unwin, London, 1989
–. *Jacques Lacan: A Feminist Introduction*, Routledge, London, 1990
–. *Volatile Bodies,* Indiana University Press, Bloomington, 1994
–. *Space, Time and Perversion*, Routledge, London, 1995

Donald Gutiervez. *Lapsing Out: Embodiments of Death and Rebirth in the Last Writings of D.H. Lawrence*, Associated University Presses 1980
E. Hahn. *Lorenzo*, Lippincott, NY, 1975
L. Hamalian, ed. *D.H. Lawrence: A Collection of Criticism*, McGraw-Hill, NY, 1973
Graham Handley. *Brodie's Notes on D.H. Lawrence's Sons and Lovers*, Pan 1976
F.C. Happold, ed. *Mysticism*, Penguin 1970
J. Harris. *The Short Fiction of D.H. Lawrence*, Rutgers University Press, New Jersey, 1984
Stephen Hazell, ed. *The English Novel*, Macmillan 1978
J. Heath. "Helen Corke and *D.H. Lawrence*", *Feminist Studies*, 11, 2, 1985
Carolyn Heilbrun. *Towards a Recognition of Androgyny*, Harper & Row, New York, 1974
R. Heppenstall. *Four Absentees*, Sphere, 1988
Christopher Heywood, ed. *D.H. Lawrence: New Studies*, Macmillan 1987
S Hignett. *Brett: From Bloomsbury to New Mexico*, Hodder, London, 1984
E. Hilton. "Alice Dax", *D.H. Lawrence Review*, 22, 3, Autumn, 1990
E.J. Hinz. "*The Rainbow*: Ursula's "Liberation"", *Contemporary Literature*, 17, 1976
—. & J.L. Teunissen. "Saviour and Cock", *Journal of Modern Literature*, 5, 1976
—. "Pornography, Novel, Mythic Narrative: The Three Versions of *Lady Chatterley's Lover*", *Modernist Studies*, 3, 1, 1979
Philip Hobsbaum. *A Reader's Guide to D.H. Lawrence*, Thames and Hudson 1981
G. Holderness. *Who's Who in D.H. Lawrence*, Hamish Hamilton, London, 1976
—. "*The Rainbow* and Organic Form", *Red Letters*, 10, 1980
—. *D.H. Lawrence*, Macmillan, London, 1982
B. Hochman. *Another Ego: D.H. Lawrence*, University of South Carolina Press, 1970
F. Hoffmann & H.T. Moore, eds. *The Achievement of D.H. Lawrence*, University of Oklahoma Press, 1953
D. Holbrook. *The Quest For Love*, Methuen, London, 1964
—. *Where D.H. Lawrence Was Wrong About Woman*, Bucknell University Press, 1992
—. "F.R. Leavis and the Erosion of His Influence", *Cambridge Review*, Nov, 1995
Graham Hough. *The Dark Sun: A Study of D.H. Lawrence*, Duckworth 1970
M. Howe. *The Art of the Self in D.H. Lawrence*, Ohio University Press, 1977
M. Oldfield Howey. *The Horse in Magic and Myth*, Castle Books, New York 1958
J.B. Humma. "More Matter, Less Art: The Continuing Course of Lawrence Criticism", *Studies in the Novel*, 19, 1, Spring, 1987
A. Huxley. *Point Counter Point*, Chatto, London, 1928
—. *Collected Essays*, Bantam, NY, 1960
—. *Letters of Aldous Huxley*, Chatto, London, 1969
G.M. Hyde. *D.H. Lawrence*, Macmillan 1990
E. Ingersoll. "The Pursuit of 'True Marriage'", *Studies in the Humanities*, 14, 1,

June 1987
—. *D.H. Lawrence, Desire and Narrative*, University of Florida Press, 2001
Allen Ingram. *The Language of D.H. Lawrence*, Macmillan 1990
K. Innis. *D.H. Lawrence's Bestiary*, Mouton, The Hague, 1971
L. Irigaray. *This Sex Which Is Not One*, tr. C. Porter & C. Burke, Cornell University Press, NY, 1977
—. *Speculum of the Other Woman*, tr. G.C. Gill, Cornell University Press, NY, 1985
—. *The Irigaray Reader*, ed. M. Whitford, Blackwell, Oxford, 1991
D. Jackson. ""The Old Pagan Vision"", *D.H. Lawrence Review*, 11, 3, 1978
—. ed. *The D.H. Lawrence Review*, University of Delaware, Newark, various issues, including 8, 3, Autumn, 1975 (*D.H. Lawrence and Women* issue)
—. & F. B. Jackson, eds. *Critical Essays on D.H. Lawrence*, G.K. Hall, Boston, 1988
R. Jackson. *Frieda Lawrence*, Pandora, London, 1994
Martin Jarret-Kerr. *D.H. Lawrence and Human Existence*, SCM Press 1961
William M. Jones. "Growth of a Symbol: The Sun in D.H. Lawrence and Eudora Welty", *University of Kansas City Review*, 26, no. 1, 1959, 68-73
N. Joost & A. Sullivan. *D.H. Lawrence and 'The Dial'*, Feffer & Simons, 1970
C.G. Jung. *Memories, Dreams, Reflections*, Collins 1967
M. Kalnins, ed. *D.H. Lawrence: Centenary Essays*, Bristol Classical Press, 1986
Nigel Kelsey. *D.H. Lawrence: Sexual Crisis*, Macmillan 1991
D. Kenmare. *D.H. Lawrence*, Barrie, London, 1951
F. Kermode. *Lawrence*, Fontana, London, 1973
Robert Kiely. "Accident And Purpose: "Bad Form" in Lawrence's Fiction", in P. Balbert, 91-107
—. *D.H. Lawrence: Triumph to Exile, 1912-1922*, Cambridge University Press, Cambridge, 1996
Mark Kinkead-Weekes, ed. *Twentieth-Century Interpretations of The Rainbow*, Prentice-Hall, New Jersey 1971
Bettina L.Knapp. *Anaïs Nin*, Frederick Ungar Publishing, New York 1978
G. Wilson Knight. *Neglected Powers*, Routledge & Kegan Paul 1972
Cheris Kramarae & Paula A. Treichler, eds. *A Feminist Dictionary*, Pandora Press, 1987
J. Kristeva. *Desire in Language: A Semiotic Approach to Literature and Art*, ed. L. Roudiez, tr. T. Gora *et al*, Blackwell, 1982
—. *The Kristeva Reader*, ed. T. Moi, Blackwell, 1986
—. *Tales of Love*, tr. L. Roudicz, Columbia University Press, NY, 1987
—. *Powers of Horror: An Essay on Abjection*, tr. L. Roudiez, Columbia University Press, NY, 1982
—. *Revolution in Poetic Language*, tr. M. Walker, Columbia University Press, NY, 1984
R.J. Kuczkowski. *Lawrence's "Esoteric" Psychology*, University Microfilms, Ann Arbor, 1974
Weston La Barre. *The Ghost Dance*, Allen & Unwin 1972
—. *Muelos*, Columbia University Press, New York 1985
Jacques Lacan and the Ecole Freudienne. *Feminine Sexuality*, ed. Juliet

Mitchell and Jacqueline Rose, Macmillan 1988
Marghanita Laski. *Ecstasy*, Cresset Press 1961
A. Lawrence & G.S. Gelder. *The Early Life of D.H. Lawrence*, Secker, London, 1932
The D.H. Lawrence Review, ed. Dennis Jackson, University of Delaware, Newark, vol. 21, no. 2, 1989
F. Lawrence. *Frieda Lawrence: Memoirs and Correspondence*, Heinemann, London, 1961
—. *Not I, But the Wind*, Granada, London, 1985
F.E. Lea. *The Life of John Middleton Murry*, London, 1959
F.R. Leavis. *D.H. Lawrence*, Minority Press, Cambridge, 1930
—. *D.H. Lawrence: Novelist*, Penguin, London, 1964
—. *Thought, Words and Creativity: Art and Thought in Lawrence*, Oxford University Press, Oxford, 1976
L. Lerner. *The Truthtellers: Austen, Eliot, Lawrence*, Chatto, London, 1967
G. Levine. *The Realistic Imagination: English Fiction From Frankenstein to Lady Chatterley*, University of Chicago Press, 1981
J.C.F. Littlewood. *D.H. Lawrence: I: 1885-1914*, British Council/ Longmans 1976
David Lodge. *Language of Fiction*, Routledge & Kegan Paul 1966
R. Lucas. *Frieda Lawrence*, Viking, London, 1973
M.D. Luhan. *Lorenzo in Taos*, Secker, London, 1933
—. *Intimate Memories*, Secker, London, 1933
—. *Intimate Memories*, Harcourt, Brace, NY, 1933/5
F. MacCarthy. *Eric Gill*, Faber, London, 1989
Sheila Macleod. *Lawrence's Men and Women*, Heinemann 1985
Neil McEwan. *D.H. Lawrence: Selected Short Stories*, Longman 1991
B. Maddox. *The Married Man: A Life of D.H. Lawrence*, Sinclair-Stevenson, London, 1994
Norman Mailer. *The Prisoner of Sex*, New American Library/ Signet 1971
K. Mansfield. *The Letters of Katherine Mansfield*, London, 1928
—. *Katherine Mansfield's Letters to John Middleton Murry*, London, 1951
—. *The Collected Letters of Katherine Mansfield*, Oxford, 1984
E. Marks & I. de Courtivron, eds. *New French Feminisms: an anthology*, Harvester Wheatsheaf, 1981
Keith M. May. *Nietzsche and Modern Literature: Themes in Yeats, Rilke, Mann and Lawrence*, Macmillan 1988
J. Mandel. "Medieval Romance and *Lady Chatterley's Lover*", *D.H. Lawrence Review*, 10, 1, 1977
N. McEwan. *D.H. Lawrence: Selected Short Stories*, Longman, London, 1991
Patricia Merivale. *Pan the Goat-God: His Myth in Modern Times*, Harvard University Press, Mass., 1969
K. Merrild. *A Poet and Two Painters*, Viking, London, 1939
—. *With D.H. Lawrence in New Mexico*, Routledge, London, 1964
J.C.J. Metford. *Dictionary of Christian Lore and Legend*, Thames & Hudson 1983
J. Meyers. *Painting and the Novel*, Manchester University Press, 1975

—. ed. *Homosexuality and Literature 1890-1930*, London, 1977
—. *Memoirs of D.H. Lawrence, D.H. Lawrence Review*, 14, 1, Spring, 1981
—. *D.H. Lawrence and the Experience of Italy*, Philadelphia, 1982
—. ed. *D.H. Lawrence and Tradition*, Athlone Press, London, 1985
—. ed. *The Legacy of D.H. Lawrence: New Essays*, Macmillan, London, 1987
—. *D.H. Lawrence*, Knopf, NY, 1990
J. Michaels-Tonks. *D.H. Lawrence: The Polarity of North and South*, Bouvier, Bonn, 1976
S. Miko, ed. *20th Century Interpretations of 'Women in Love'*, Prentice-Hall, 1969
—. *Toward Women in Love: The Emergence of a Lawrentian Aesthetic*, Yale University Press, New Haven, 1971
K.M. Miles. *The Hellish Meaning: D.H. Lawrence*, Southern Illinois University Press, Carbondale, 1969
T.H. Miles. "Birkin's Electro-Mystical Body of Reality", *D.H. Lawrence*, 9, 1976
Henry Miller. *The World of Lawrence: A Passionate Appreciation*, ed. Evelyn J. Hinz & John J. Teunissen, Calder 1985
Kate Millett. *Sexual Politics*, Doubleday, Garden City 1970
S. Milligan. *Lady Chatterley's Lover According To Spike Milligan*, Penguin, 1995
Colin Milton. *Lawrence and Nietzsche: A Study in Influence*, Aberdeen University Press 1987
H.T. Moore. *Poste Restante: A Lawrence Travel Calendar*, University of California Press, Berkeley, 1956
—. ed. *A D.H. Lawrence Miscellany*, Southern Illinois University Press, Carbondale, 1959
—. *The Intelligent Heart: The Story of D.H. Lawrence*, Penguin, London, 1960
—. *D.H. Lawrence: The Life and Works*, Twayne, 1964
—. *The Priest of Love: A Life of D.H. Lawrence*, Penguin, London, 1976
—. & W. Roberts. *D.H. Lawrence and His World*, Thames and Hudson, London, 1966/88
R. Montgomery. *The Visionary D.H. Lawrence*, Cambridge University Press, Cambridge, 1994
H. Mori, ed. *A Conversation on D.H. Lawrence*, UCLA Library, LA, 1974
Lady O. Morrell. *Ottoline at Garsington: Memoirs, 1915-1918*, ed. R. Gathorne-Hardy, Faber, London, 1974
J. Moynahan. *The Deed of Life: The Novels and Tales of D.H. Lawrence*, Princeton University Press, New Jersey, 1966
—. ed. *'Sons and Lovers': Text, Background, and Criticism*, Viking, London, 1968
R.C. Murfin. *Swinburne, Hardy, Lawrence sand the Burden of Belief*, University of Chicago Press, 1978
J.M. Murry. review, *Nation and Athenaeum*, 29, Aug, 1921
—. review, *Adelphi*, 2, June, 1929
—. *D.H. Lawrence*, Minority Press, Cambridge, 1930
—. *Son of Woman: The Story of D.H. Lawrence*, Cape, 1931
—. *Reminiscences of D.H. Lawrence*, Cape, London, 1933

—. *Love, Freedom and Society*, Cape, London, 1957
—. *The Letters of John Middleton Murry to Katherine Manfield*, London, 1983
C. Nahal. *D.H. Lawrence: An Eastern View*, Barnes, NY, 1970
Edward Nehls, ed. *D.H. Lawrence: A Composite Biography*, 3 vols, University of Wisconsin Press, Madison 1958
G. Neville. *A Memoir of D.H. Lawrence*, Cambridge University Press, Cambridge, 1981
Erich Neumann. *The Great Mother*, Princeton University Press, New Jersey 1972
Shirley Nicholson, ed. *The Goddess Re-awakening*, Theosophical Publishing House, New York 1989
Friedrich Nietzsche. *Beyond Good and Evil*, tr. Zimmern, Allen & Unwin 1907/67
—. *A Nietzsche Reader*, ed. R.J. Hollingdale, Penguin 1977
Anaïs Nin. *The Novel of the Future*, Collier/ Macmillan, New York 1970
—. *D.H. Lawrence: An Unprofessional Study*, Black Spring 1985
Alistair Niven. *D.H. Lawrence: The Novels*, Cambridge University Press 1978
Carol Nixon. *Lawrence's Leadership Politics and the Turn Against Women*, University of California Press, Berkeley 1986
Wendy O'Flaherty. *Women, Androgynes, and Other Mythical Beasts*, University of Chicago Press, Chicago 1980
Daniel O'Hara. "The Power of Nothing in *Women In Love*", *Bucknell Review: A Scholarly Journal of Letters, Arts and Science*, ed. Harry R. Garvin, 28, 1983, and in P. Widdowson, 146-159
N. Page. *D.H. Lawrence*, Macmillan, London, 1981
G. Panichas. *Adventures in the Consciousness: The Meaning of D.H. Lawrence's Religious Quest*, Mouton, The Hague, 1964
—. *The Reverent Discipline*, University of Tennessee Press, Knoxville, TN, 1974
D. Parker. "Lawrence and Lady Chatterley", *Critical Review*, 20, 1978
Robert B. Partlow & Harry T. Moore, eds. *D.H. Lawrence: The Man Who Lived*, Southern Illinois University Press, Carbondale 1980
F.B. Pinion. *A D.H. Lawrence Companion: Life, Thought and Works*, Macmillan 1978
Tony Pinkey. *D.H. Lawrence*, Harvester Press 1990
V. de S. Pinto. *D.H. Lawrence*, Nottingham, 1951
—. *D.H. Lawrence After 30 Years*, Nottingham, 1960
R. Poole. "Psychoanalytic Theory: *St Mawr*", in Tallack, 1987
P. Poplawski, ed. *Writing the Body of D.H. Lawrence*, Greenwood Press, 2001
K. Porter. "A Wreath For the Gamekeeper" *Encounter*, Feb, 1960
S. Potter. *D.H. Lawrence*, Cape, London, 1930
John Cowper Powys. *Autobiography*, Macdonald 1967
—. In *Defence of Sensuality*, Gollancz 1930
J.S. Poynter, ed. *Journal of the D.H. Lawrence Society*, D.H. Lawrence Society of the UK, London, 1976-
Peter Preston & Peter Hoare, eds. *D.H. Lawrence in the Modern World*, Macmillan 1989
R.E. Pritchard. *D.H. Lawrence: Body of Darkness*, Hutchinson 1971

Michael Ragussis. *The Subterfuge of Art*, John Hopkins University Press, Baltimore 1978

R. Rees. *D.H. Lawrence*, Gollancz, London, 1958

C. Rembar. *The End of Obscenity: The Trials of Lady Chatterley's Lover, Tropic of Cancer, and Fanny Hill*, Randhom House, 1968

J.A. Roberts. *The Shakespearean Wild: Geography, Genus and Gender*, University of Nebraska Press, Lincoln, Nebraska 1991

W. Roberts. *A Bibliography of D.H. Lawrence*, Rupert Hart-Davis, 1963/ Cambridge University Press, Cambridge, 1982

Jeremy Robinson. *The Passion of D.H. Lawrence*, Crescent Moon 1992

C.H. Rolph, ed. *The Trial of Lady Chatterley: Regina v. Penguin Books Limited*, Penguin, London, 1961

—. *The Composition of "The Rainbow" and "Women in Love": A History*, University Press of Virginia, Charlottesville, VI, 1979

Charles L. Ross. *The Composition of "The Rainbow" and "Women In Love": A History*, University Press of Virginia, Charlottesville 1979

—. "The Revisions of the Second Generation in *The Rainbow*", *Review of English Studies*, 27, 1976, 277-95

J. Ruderman. "*Women in Love*", *Mosaic*, Winter, 1982

—. *D.H. Lawrence and the Devouring Mother*, Duke University Press, Durham, NC, 1984

Bertrand Russell. *A History of Western Philosophy*, Allen & Unwin 1971

K. Sagar. *The Art of D.H. Lawrence*, Cambridge University Press, Cambridge, 1966

—. "The Genesis of *The Rainbow* and *Women in Love*", *D.H. Lawrence Review*, 1, 1968

—. *D.H. Lawrence: A Calendar of His Works*, Manchester University Press, 1979

—. *The Life of D.H. Lawrence: An Illustrated Biography*, Eyre Methuen, London, 1980

—. *A D.H. Lawrence Handbook*, Manchester University Press, 1982

—. *Life Into Art*, Viking, London, 1985

—. *D. H. Lawrence and New Mexico*, Alyscamps Press, Paris, 1995

G. Salgado. *A Preface to Lawrence*, Longman, London, 1982

—. ed. *D.H. Lawrence: Sons and Lovers: A Casebook*, Macmillan, London, 1969

—. & G.R. Das, eds. *The Spirit of D.H. Lawrence: Centenary Studies*, Macmillan, London, 1988

R. Sale. "The Narrative Technique of *The Rainbow*", *Modern Fiction Studies*, 5, Spring, 1959

—. *Modern Heroism*, University of California Press, Berkeley, 1973

Gamini Salgado. *A Preface to Lawrence*, Longman 1982

—. ed. *D.H. Lawrence: Sons and Lovers: A Casebook*, Macmillan 1969

—. and G.R. Das, eds. *The Spirit of D.H. Lawrence: Centenary Studies*, Macmillan 1988

Scott Sanders. *D. H. Lawrence: The World of the Major Works*, Vision Press 1973

B. Schapiro. *D.H. Lawrence and the Paradoxes of Psychic Life*, State

University of New York Press, 1999
P. Scheckner. *Class, Politics and the Individual: A Study of the Major Novels of D.H. Lawrence*, Farleigh Dickinson University Press, N.J., 1985
D.J. Schneider. *D.H. Lawrence: The Artist as Psychologist*, University Press of Kansas, Lawrence, 1984
—. *The Consciousness of D.H. Lawrence*, University Press of Kansas, Lawrence, 1986
M. Schorer. *D.H. Lawrence*, Dell, NY, 1968
H.J. Seligmann. *D.H. Lawrence*, Seltzer, NY, 1924
Penelope Shuttle & Peter Redgrove. *The Wise Wound*, Paladin/ Grafton 1978/ 86
M. Shaw. "Lawrence and Feminism", *Critical Quarterly*, 25, 3, 1983
Carol Siegel. *Lawrence Among the Women: Wavering Boundaries in Women's Literary Tradition*, University Press of Virginia, Charlottesville 1991
Hilary Simpson. *D.H. Lawrence and Feminism*, Croom Helm 1982
A. Sitesh. *D.H. Lawrence*, Macmillan, London, 1975
Sylvia Skylar. *The Plays of D.H. Lawrence*, Vision Press 1975
Tony Slade. *D.H. Lawrence*, Evans Brothers Ltd 1969
Anne Smith, ed. *Lawrence and Women*, Vision Press 1978
Frank G. Smith. *D.H. Lawrence: The Rainbow*, Edward Arnold 1971
Hilda Spear. *York Notes: D.H. Lawrence: The Rainbow*, York Press, Harlow 1991
Stephen Spender, ed. *D.H. Lawrence: Novelist, Poet, Prophet*, Weidenfeld & Nicolson 1973
M. Spilka, ed. *D.H. Lawrence: A Collection of Critical Essays*, Prentice-Hall, New Jersey, 1963
—. *The Love Ethic of D.H. Lawrence*, Indiana University Press, Bloomington, 1955
—. "Lawrence Up-Tight, or the Anal Phase Once Over", *Novel*, 4, 3, Spring, 1971
M. Squires. *The Pastoral Novel: Studies in George Eliot, Thomas Hardy and D.H. Lawrence*, University Press of Virginia, Charlottesville, 1974
—. *The Creation of Lady Chatterley's Lover*, Johns Hopkins University Press, 1983
—. & D. Jackson, eds. *D.H. Lawrence's Lady: A New Look at Lady Chatterley's Lover*, University of Georgia Press, Athens, 1985
—. & K. Cushman, eds. *The Challenge of D.H. Lawrence*, University of Wisconsin Press, Madison, 1990
—. & K. Cushman, eds. *D.H. Lawrence Manuscripts*, St Martin's Press, NY, 1991
Garrett Stewart. "Lawrence, 'Being' and the Allotropic Style", *Novel*, 9, 1976, 217-42
K. Stewart. *The Vitality of D.H. Lawrence*, Southern Illinois University Press, 2000
T. Stoehr. "'Mentalized Sex" in D.H Lawrence", *Novel*, 8, 1975
J.E. Stoll. *The Novels of D.H. Lawrence*, University of Missouri Press, Columbia, 1971
—. *D.H. Lawrence: A Bibliography 1911-1975*, Whitson, NY, 1977
G. Strickland. "The First *Lady Chatterley's Lover*", *Encounter*, 36, Jan, 1971

P. Stubbs. *Women and Fiction: Feminism and the Novel, 1880-1920,* Harvester, 1979
Richard Swigg. *Lawrence, Hardy and American Literature,* Oxford University Press 1972
D. Tallack, ed. *Literary Theory At Work,* Batsford, London, 1987
E.W. Tedlock. *The Frieda Lawrence Collection of D.H. Lawrence Manuscripts,* University of New Mexico Press, Albuquerque, 1948
—. *D.H. Lawrence,* University of New Mexico Press, Albuquerque, 1963
—. ed. *D.H. Lawrence and 'Sons and Lovers',* New York University Press, 1963
W.Y. Tindall. *D.H. Lawrence and Susan His Cow,* Columbia University Press, 1939
—. *The Later D.H. Lawrence,* Knopf, NY, 1852
G. Trease. *D.H. Lawrence,* Macmillan, London, 1973
D.W. Veitch. *Lawrence, Greene and Lowry,* Waterloo, Ontario, 1978
E. Vivas. *D.H. Lawrence: The Failure and the Triumph of Love,* Indiana University Press, Bloomington, 1960
D.A. Weiss. *Oedipus in Nottingham: D.H. Lawrence,* University of Washington Press, Seattle, 1962
A. West. *D.H. Lawrence,* Barker, London, 1966
R. West. *D.H. Lawrence,* Secker, London, 1930
P.T. Whelan. *D.H. Lawrence,* UMI Research Press, Ann Arbor, 1988
W. White. *D.H. Lawrence,* Wayne state University Press, Detroit, 1950
Peter Widdowson. *Hardy in History: A study in literary sociology,* Routledge 1989
K. Widmer. "Lawrence and the Fall of Modern Woman", *Modern Fiction Studies,* 5, 1959
—. *The Art of Perversity: D.H. Lawrence's Shorter Fictions,* University of Washington Press, 1962
—. "The Pertinence of Modern Pastoral: The Three Versions of *Lady Chatterley's Lover*", *Studies in the Novel,* 5, 1973
L.R. Williams. "The Trial of D.H. Lawrence", *Critical Survey,* Spring, 1992
—. *Critical Desire: Psychoanalysis and the Literary Subject,* Arnold, London, 1995a
—. *Sex in the Head: Visions of Femininity in D.H. Lawrence,* Harvester Wheatsheaf, 1995b
—. *D.H. Lawrence, Writers and Their Works,* Northcote House, 1997
Merryn Williams. *Thomas Hardy and Rural England,* Macmillan 1972
R. Williams. *The English Novel From Dickens to Lawrence,* Chatto, London, 1970
Colin Wilson. *The Sexual Misfits: A Study of Sexual Outsiders,* Collins 1989
J. Wilt. *Ghosts of the Gothic: Austen, Eliot and Lawrence,* Princeton University Press, 1980
J. Worthen. *D.H. Lawrence and the Idea of the Novel,* Macmillan, 1979
—. *D.H. Lawrence: A Literary Life,* Macmillan, 1989
—. *D.H. Lawrence,* Arnold, London, 1991a
—. *D.H. Lawrence: The Early Years, 1885-1912,* Cambridge University Press, Cambridge, 1991b

M. Yorke. *Eric Gill: Man of Flesh and Spirit*, Constable 1981
Kenneth Young. *D.H. Lawrence*, British Council/ Longmans 1969
Yudhishtar. *Conflict in the Novels of D.H. Lawrence*, Oliver & Boyd, London, 1969
A.L. Zambrano. *"Women in Love", Literature/ Film Quarterly*, 1, Jan, 1973
Jack Zipes. *The Brothers Grimm: From Enchanted Forests to the Modern World*, Routledge 1989
G. Zytaruk. *D.H. Lawrence's Response to Russian Literature*, Mouton, The Hague, 1971
—. "The Phallic Vision: D.H. Lawrence and V.V. Rozanov", *Comparative Literature Studies*, 4, 3, 1967

WEBSITES

D.H. Lawrence Society of North America   dhlsna.bravesites.com
D.H. Lawrence Society (G.B.)   dhlawrence.com
D.H. Lawrence Research Centre
D.H. Lawrence Society (Australia)   dhlawrencesocietyaustralia.com.au
D.H. Lawrence Review   dhlawrencereview.org

CRESCENT MOON PUBLISHING

web: www.crmoon.com e-mail: cresmopub@yahoo.co.uk

ARTS, PAINTING, SCULPTURE

The Art of Andy Goldsworthy
Andy Goldsworthy: Touching Nature
Andy Goldsworthy in Close-Up
Andy Goldsworthy: Pocket Guide
Andy Goldsworthy In America
Land Art: A Complete Guide
The Art of Richard Long
Richard Long: Pocket Guide
Land Art In the UK
Land Art in Close-Up
Land Art In the U.S.A.
Land Art: Pocket Guide
Installation Art in Close-Up
Minimal Art and Artists In the 1960s and After
Colourfield Painting
Land Art DVD, TV documentary
Andy Goldsworthy DVD, TV documentary
The Erotic Object: Sexuality in Sculpture From Prehistory to the Present Day
Sex in Art: Pornography and Pleasure in Painting and Sculpture
Postwar Art
Sacred Gardens: The Garden in Myth, Religion and Art
Glorification: Religious Abstraction in Renaissance and 20th Century Art
Early Netherlandish Painting
Leonardo da Vinci
Piero della Francesca
Giovanni Bellini
Fra Angelico: Art and Religion in the Renaissance
Mark Rothko: The Art of Transcendence
Frank Stella: American Abstract Artist
Jasper Johns
Brice Marden
Alison Wilding: The Embrace of Sculpture
Vincent van Gogh: Visionary Landscapes
Eric Gill: Nuptials of God
Constantin Brancusi: Sculpting the Essence of Things
Max Beckmann
Caravaggio
Gustave Moreau
Egon Schiele: Sex and Death In Purple Stockings
Delizioso Fotografico Fervore: Works In Process 1
Sacro Cuore: Works In Process 2
The Light Eternal: J.M.W. Turner
The Madonna Glorified: Karen Arthurs

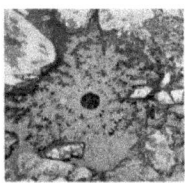

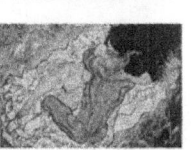

LITERATURE

J.R.R. Tolkien: The Books, The Films, The Whole Cultural Phenomenon
J.R.R. Tolkien: Pocket Guide
Tolkien's Heroic Quest
The *Earthsea* Books of Ursula Le Guin
Beauties, Beasts and Enchantment: Classic French Fairy Tales
German Popular Stories by the Brothers Grimm
Philip Pullman and *His Dark Materials*
Sexing Hardy: Thomas Hardy and Feminism
Thomas Hardy's *Tess of the d'Urbervilles*
Thomas Hardy's *Jude the Obscure*
Thomas Hardy: The Tragic Novels
Love and Tragedy: Thomas Hardy
The Poetry of Landscape in Hardy
Wessex Revisited: Thomas Hardy and John Cowper Powys
Wolfgang Iser: Essays and Interviews
Petrarch, Dante and the Troubadours
Maurice Sendak and the Art of Children's Book Illustration
Andrea Dworkin
Cixous, Irigaray, Kristeva: The *Jouissance* of French Feminism
Julia Kristeva: Art, Love, Melancholy, Philosophy, Semiotics and Psychoanalysis
Hélene Cixous I Love You: The *Jouissance* of Writing
Luce Irigaray: Lips, Kissing, and the Politics of Sexual Difference
Peter Redgrove: Here Comes the Flood
Peter Redgrove: Sex-Magic-Poetry-Cornwall
Lawrence Durrell: Between Love and Death, East and West
Love, Culture & Poetry: Lawrence Durrell
Cavafy: Anatomy of a Soul
German Romantic Poetry: Goethe, Novalis, Heine, Hölderlin
Feminism and Shakespeare
Shakespeare: Love, Poetry & Magic
The Passion of D.H. Lawrence
D.H. Lawrence: Symbolic Landscapes
D.H. Lawrence: Infinite Sensual Violence
Rimbaud: Arthur Rimbaud and the Magic of Poetry
The Ecstasies of John Cowper Powys
Sensualism and Mythology: The Wessex Novels of John Cowper Powys
Amorous Life: John Cowper Powys and the Manifestation of Affectivity (H.W. Fawkner)
Postmodern Powys: New Essays on John Cowper Powys (Joe Boulter)
Rethinking Powys: Critical Essays on John Cowper Powys
Paul Bowles & Bernardo Bertolucci
Rainer Maria Rilke
Joseph Conrad: *Heart of Darkness*
In the Dim Void: Samuel Beckett
Samuel Beckett Goes into the Silence
André Gide: Fiction and Fervour
Jackie Collins and the Blockbuster Novel
Blinded By Her Light: The Love-Poetry of Robert Graves
The Passion of Colours: Travels In Mediterranean Lands
Poetic Forms

POETRY

Ursula Le Guin: Walking In Cornwall
Peter Redgrove: Here Comes The Flood
Peter Redgrove: Sex-Magic-Poetry-Cornwall
Dante: Selections From the Vita Nuova
Petrarch, Dante and the Troubadours
William Shakespeare: Sonnets
William Shakespeare: Complete Poems
Blinded By Her Light: The Love-Poetry of Robert Graves
Emily Dickinson: Selected Poems
Emily Brontë: Poems
Thomas Hardy: Selected Poems
Percy Bysshe Shelley: Poems
John Keats: Selected Poems
Joh n Keats: Poems of 1820
D.H. Lawrence: Selected Poems
Edmund Spenser: Poems
Edmund Spenser: Amoretti
John Donne: Poems
Henry Vaughan: Poems
Sir Thomas Wyatt: Poems
Robert Herrick: Selected Poems
Rilke: Space, Essence and Angels in the Poetry of Rainer Maria Rilke
Rainer Maria Rilke: Selected Poems
Friedrich Hölderlin: Selected Poems
Arseny Tarkovsky: Selected Poems
Arthur Rimbaud: Selected Poems
Arthur Rimbaud: A Season in Hell
Arthur Rimbaud and the Magic of Poetry
Novalis: Hymns To the Night
German Romantic Poetry
Paul Verlaine: Selected Poems
Elizaethan Sonnet Cycles
D.J. Enright: By-Blows
Jeremy Reed: Brigitte's Blue Heart
Jeremy Reed: Claudia Schiffer's Red Shoes
Gorgeous Little Orpheus
Radiance: New Poems
Crescent Moon Book of Nature Poetry
Crescent Moon Book of Love Poetry
Crescent Moon Book of Mystical Poetry
Crescent Moon Book of Elizabethan Love Poetry
Crescent Moon Book of Metaphysical Poetry
Crescent Moon Book of Romantic Poetry
Pagan America: New American Poetry

MEDIA, CINEMA, FEMINISM and CULTURAL STUDIES

J.R.R. Tolkien: The Books, The Films, The Whole Cultural Phenomenon
J.R.R. Tolkien: Pocket Guide
The *Lord of the Rings* Movies: Pocket Guide
The Cinema of Hayao Miyazaki
Hayao Miyazaki: *Princess Mononoke*: Pocket Movie Guide
Hayao Miyazaki: *Spirited Away*: Pocket Movie Guide
Tim Burton : Hallowe'en For Hollywood
Ken Russell
Ken Russell: *Tommy*: Pocket Movie Guide
The Ghost Dance: The Origins of Religion
The Peyote Cult
Cixous, Irigaray, Kristeva: The *Jouissance* of French Feminism
Julia Kristeva: Art, Love, Melancholy, Philosophy, Semiotics and Psychoanalysis
Luce Irigaray: Lips, Kissing, and the Politics of Sexual Difference
Hélene Cixous I Love You: The *Jouissance* of Writing
Andrea Dworkin
'Cosmo Woman': The World of Women's Magazines
Women in Pop Music
HomeGround: The Kate Bush Anthology
Discovering the Goddess (Geoffrey Ashe)
The Poetry of Cinema
The Sacred Cinema of Andrei Tarkovsky
Andrei Tarkovsky: Pocket Guide
Andrei Tarkovsky: *Mirror*: Pocket Movie Guide
Andrei Tarkovsky: *The Sacrifice*: Pocket Movie Guide
Walerian Borowczyk: Cinema of Erotic Dreams
Jean-Luc Godard: The Passion of Cinema
Jean-Luc Godard: *Hail Mary*: Pocket Movie Guide
Jean-Luc Godard: *Contempt*: Pocket Movie Guide
Jean-Luc Godard: *Pierrot le Fou*: Pocket Movie Guide
John Hughes and Eighties Cinema
Ferris Bueller's Day Off: Pocket Movie Guide
Jean-Luc Godard: Pocket Guide
The Cinema of Richard Linklater
Liv Tyler: Star In Ascendance
Blade Runner and the Films of Philip K. Dick
Paul Bowles and Bernardo Bertolucci
Media Hell: Radio, TV and the Press
An Open Letter to the BBC
Detonation Britain: Nuclear War in the UK
Feminism and Shakespeare
Wild Zones: Pornography, Art and Feminism
Sex in Art: Pornography and Pleasure in Painting and Sculpture
Sexing Hardy: Thomas Hardy and Feminism

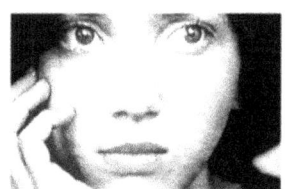

The Light Eternal is a model monograph, an exemplary job. The subject matter of the book is beautifully organised and dead on beam. (Lawrence Durrell)
It is amazing for me to see my work treated with such passion and respect. (Andrea Dworkin)

CRESCENT MOON PUBLISHING
P.O. Box 1312, Maidstone, Kent, ME14 5XU, Great Britain. www.crmoon.com

cresmopub@yahoo.co.uk   www.crescentmoon.org.uk

www.ingramcontent.com/pod-product-compliance
Lightning Source LLC
Chambersburg PA
CBHW070149100426
42743CB00013B/2856